<small>THE</small> Amateurs

THE
Amateurs
David Halberstam

Hodder & Stoughton
LONDON SYDNEY AUCKLAND TORONTO

British Library Cataloguing in Publication Data

Halberstam, David
   The amateurs.
   1. Rowers – United States – Biography
   I. Title
   797.1′23′0922   GV790.9

   ISBN 0 340 39642 3

For Mary Ann Madden

THEAmateurs

CHAPTER
ONE

It was not a celebrated event. It was an Olympic trial, to be sure, and the trial of a sport of unusually passionate participants. But no tickets were sold, and the community in which it was held, Princeton, New Jersey, largely ignored it. The local innkeepers and restaurateurs did not report to the Chamber of Commerce, as seems mandatory these days, that holding the sculling finals in their city had brought $5 million worth of extra business to the town. A handful of hastily put up cardboard signs told the curious few how to find their way through Princeton's streets to the shores of Lake Carnegie. In a world of media events, journalists were notably absent. There were no press credentials; there were no television cameras; there was only one still photographer on duty. One young woman from the U.S. Rowing Association was in charge of the press, and her typewriter, old and battered, immediately broke down. A reporter from the *Boston Globe* showed, and so did one from the *Philadelphia Inquirer*. Those papers probably represented the two most serious rowing cities in America; Harvard-Penn rivalries in crew were special. *The New York Times* sent a stringer; crew was a shakier sport at Columbia. The regional Associated Press bureaus seemed to be competing for the right *not* to cover it.

The scullers of America existed, it was clear, in a world of their own.

No chartered planes or buses ferried the athletes into Princeton. No team managers hustled their baggage from the bus to the hotel desk and made arrangements so that at mealtime they need only show up and sign the tab. This was a world of hitched rides and borrowed beds, and meals, if not scrounged, were desperately budgeted by appallingly hungry young men. The rowers were *always* hungry. Food was fuel, and they burned immense amounts of fuel, judging restaurants not by quality but by quantity.

Christopher Wood of Cambridge, Massachusetts, the favorite to win the right to represent the United States in the single sculls, was particularly experienced in scrounging lodging and food, and he knew the Princeton area well. At the Princeton Motor Lodge, for example, while rowing in a four-man boat, he and his teammates had rented a double room for $30, taken the mattresses off the box springs, laid them side by side and four people had stayed in one room for $7.50 each. On this weekend Tiff Wood (from a boyhood inability to say his own name, which had come out not Christopher, but Tiffer) drove down from Cambridge with a friend and competitor named Charley Altekruse, both of their sculls strapped on Wood's car. That allowed them both to cut costs on travel. Gas, oil, meals had come to $150 for Wood, or about twice what he had gotten in expense money from the Olympic committee.

Wood liked Charley Altekruse, they were Harvard oarsmen from different crews, and Wood thought that among his colleagues Altekruse had the greatest natural athletic talent, that unlike most rowers, he would be good at almost any sport. Most scullers loved to train but hated to race because the pain and the tension of a race were so great. Wood was amused that the gifted Altekruse loved to race and hated to train. Besides, there was an additional financial benefit in traveling with Altekruse. Since he had only recently graduated from college, he had a better network of friends and graduate students planted around the eastern colleges where regattas took place. In Princeton they would stay at the home of friends of his, further saving on costs.

Tiff Wood was a champion single-scull rower, perhaps, some thought, the best American hope for a sculling Olympic medal in the 1984 games. At thirty-one he was, as a man who had devoted his entire grown life to rowing, the person-ification of the amateur. He had put aside career, marriage, pleasure in his single-minded pursuit of excellence in a sport that few of his fellow countrymen cared about and that was, therefore, absolutely without commercial rewards. Not only was he probably the official favorite for the race, he was, in the world of oarsmen, the sentimental favorite as well. As a much younger, less experienced oarsman he had been a spare on the 1976 Olympic team. But no one had become sick, and he had not rowed a stroke. A more senior figure in the world of rowing, he had been the captain of the men on the 1980 team, but Jimmy Carter had canceled U.S. partici-pation in the summer Olympics that year, and again Wood had not rowed a stroke. Because the Olympics were the one occasion when the oarsmen had a chance at national expo-sure, the boycott had been a particularly bitter blow. Wood had been their spokesman that year and had been extremely critical of Carter's decision; other athletes were privately as critical but, fearing commercial reprisals, remained publicly supportive. The oarsmen feared no reprisals to careers that had no commercial potential to begin with. So wearing their dissent as publicly as possible, they had formed a rowdy and raucous bunch during the ceremonies held in their honor in Washington by Carter. Many, like Wood, had refused to shake Carter's hand on the evening of the gala. There had even been a certain ritual for snubbing the President of the United States; those who had decided not to shake Carter's hand simply did not go onstage with him. That part at least was relatively genteel. When the ceremonies were over, most of Wood's contemporaries on the 1980 rowing team had swallowed their disappointment, vowed never to vote for Carter if he ran for reelection, and withdrawn from competitive rowing. But Wood was different. The Olympic goal had continued to tantalize him. Because, without a chance to compete in the Olympics, his rowing career seemed incomplete, he had decided to stay with the sport for one more shot, the 1984 Olympics. He loved rowing—it, more than his professional life, was his real world; and he had given a great deal personally to it, serving on various official rowing committees. Within the world of former oarsmen, there was a subtle sense that, all things being equal, it would be a nice thing if Tiff Wood won.

On this weekend, two of Wood's principal opponents, John Biglow and Joe Bouscaren, both former Yale oarsmen, had driven down together. They had rowed in an informal race the previous Sunday on the Charles against Tiff, and both had beaten him. For Bouscaren, who had come in second, the victory over Wood was a special boost. Bouscaren was a talented and graceful oar who was somewhat smaller than both Biglow and Wood; more often than not, Bouscaren led for the first half of a race, and then Wood or Biglow passed him near the end.

For Biglow, a former two-time national champion who had been bothered by a bad back and who had not rowed well in the past year, it had been a day of genuine celebration. For the first time in a year he sensed that he might be able to try the Olympic single-scull trials after all. Unlike Bouscaren and Wood, who had spent the winter rowing on the Charles and working out in Harvard's Newell Boathouse, Biglow had returned to his native Seattle and had tried to find out what was wrong with his back. He had spent most of the winter rowing in a double with his friend Paul Enquist. That put less strain on Biglow's back, for a double was not as heavy on the individual sculler as the single, and he had gradually been able to compete again. His rowing, which had been quite rough in 1983, had begun to improve. He and Enquist had formed a very good double, and there was a chance that they might become the U.S. double scull in the Olympics.

He had come back to Cambridge in mid-April resigned to the fact that if he made the Olympic team it would be in a double or a quad (a double scull was two scullers with two oars each, a quad was four scullers with two oars each, each boat without a coxswain). That was all right, he would still be part of the Olympic ideal, but in his heart he coveted the chance to be the single sculler who was *the* rower for America. As Tiff Wood once pointed out, "You could be on a championship eight which won all its races, but you might only be the fiftieth-best oarsman in the country. But the single sculler is the best, and everyone in the world of rowing knows it."

When he had showed up in Cambridge, Biglow had been without his own scull. Previously he had used one belonging to Harvard, but Harry Parker, the Olympic sculling coach, had not saved it for him and had given it instead to Altekruse. That struck Biglow as an ominous note. It was as if his place had already been taken and Harry, in his silent and almost mystical way, was no longer interested in him as a single sculler. That spring Tiff Wood had bought a brand-new scull for $3,400, had tried it out and decided he didn't like it (although he was using the seat from his new scull with his old one, which made him feel he was sitting on a $3,400 seat). Biglow had asked Wood if he would lend him the new scull. Wood, anxious to make back a little bit of the money he had just invested, had offered to rent it to him for $50 a week. That had surprised Biglow, who, just as careful with his money as Wood, had decided against renting it. Biglow had asked Harry Parker, who was also the Harvard coach, if there was an extra shell around the boathouse, and Parker had pointed to a terrible fat old boat, a loser's boat for sure. That diminished Biglow's confidence even more. At that point Biglow had thought of a sculler named Andy

Sudduth who had just ordered a new top of the line shell and then had decided to compete as a sweep oarsman instead of a sculler. Biglow had asked if he could use Sudduth's boat for a week, and Sudduth had said yes.

On the first weekend that Biglow had come back to Cambridge, Harry Parker had scheduled some informal races. On Saturday he had tried some of the oarsmen in doubles; and Biglow, who had spent the winter in a double and who had no doubt of his ability there, had been in the winning shell. On Sunday, Biglow thought he would row in a double again. But no one else wanted to row doubles, and so Parker had decided that everyone would race in singles. Parker had broken the oarsmen down into two heats. He had placed Biglow in the faster heat against Wood and Bouscaren. At first Biglow had been annoyed. He was sure that Parker was doing this to discourage him from rowing singles and trying to force him into the double. On this Sunday they would row two thousand meters, roughly a mile and a quarter, the standard distance. It was a rainy, windy day, hardly ideal for rowing, and both Bouscaren and Wood had gotten very good starts, going out quickly on Biglow. In the second five hundred they had not gained, and then, in the third five hundred meters, Biglow had begun to move. Because he was wary of pushing his back too hard, he had not gone all out. Nevertheless, in the fourth five hundred he had passed both Wood and Bouscaren. That had been Easter Sunday, and Biglow thought of it as a kind of religious experience. For the first time in a year he had been able to row at a high level without his back betraying him and his legs going numb. He had beaten his two principal competitors.

Up until that moment Harry Parker thought that John Biglow had made a commitment to the double and he had envisioned a Biglow-Enquist double as a powerful one, a likely Olympic entry. But Parker had sensed that the moment that Biglow had returned to Cambridge and smelled the Wood-Bouscaren tensions, John would be unable to resist the singles. All that ego was at stake, these were his two principal competitors from the past, it was like the third of the triplets coming home after a long trip away and wanting to play with the new toys. If Harry Parker sensed it, Paul Enquist *knew* it. "There it goes," he said to Parker on the first day, watching Biglow trailing after Wood and Bouscaren at the boathouse. After Biglow had won the singles race, Enquist had not said anything to Parker, but there was a sad look on his face. Later, when Parker had caught his eye, Enquist had shaken his head and made a downward circling motion with his right hand. The meaning was perfectly clear to Parker: Their double was down the drain.

So when John Biglow and Joe Bouscaren had driven down to Princeton together, neither thought of himself as an underdog. Biglow for the first time in a year believed his back did not hinder him, and Bouscaren believed that in the past few months he had reached virtual parity with Wood and Biglow. Bouscaren had been a year ahead of Biglow at Yale, and the two were close friends. On the way down they talked incessantly of rowing, of their bodies and of genetics. Bouscaren seemed fascinated by his body. Sports and competition obsessed him, and no one took better care of himself. He worked on his body and maximized its strength—he was smaller than the other two—and indeed at one time he had thought seriously of making sports medicine his career. He had hoped to go to Dartmouth Medical School, which was for him the perfect medical school in the perfect locale; he could row during the fall and spring and go long-distance skiing during the winter. What more could the body and the mind want? But he had not gotten in and had settled for the urban confines of Cornell Medical School in New York City. On the way down he asked Biglow whether, if he wanted to pass superior genes on to his children, he should choose a wife for her athletic ability. Was it wrong to place too much emphasis on her strength and size? Near the end of the drive, Biglow had turned to Bouscaren and said, "You know, Joe, this is the most important race of our lives." Bouscaren had been silent for a moment. "This is for the Olympics," Biglow said, "this is what we've been working for all these years. Who wins here, goes."

There was something different, almost noble about the Olympian in his mind. Four years ago he had been asked by his Yale friend and teammate Steve Kiesling why he was working so hard in preparation for the 1980 Olympics and he had answered, "the Olympian stands alone." Listening to Biglow talk about the race, Bouscaren had quietly agreed. Biglow, he knew, in his own meticulous way was already concentrating on the race, already *rowing* the race. They were both staying, fittingly enough, with a former Yale oarsman, Donald Beer, class of 1956, who had rowed in a Yale eight that had won an Olympic medal. Beer liked former Yale oarsmen to stay with him in Princeton. His house was a virtual rowing museum, replete with all kinds of souvenirs from the past. One thing above all else that John Biglow knew about the house was that there was an Olympic gold medal in it. Beer, fittingly enough, had once told Biglow, "John, always remember, there's more to life than rowing— but not much."

For the first time in almost thirty years, the United States had a serious chance to win an Olympic medal in the single sculls, albeit the bronze. For the past three years, the American scullers had taken third in the world competition. The last American Olympic single-sculls medal had been a bronze won by John Kelly, Jr., of the Philadelphia bricklaying, rowing and acting Kellys. He had taken the bronze in 1956, in his third Olympic shot (his father had won the gold in 1920 in Antwerp, the last American gold in this event). But in 1981 Biglow, then only twenty-four and rowing in his first international regatta, had surprised everyone by winning a bronze. He had repeated in 1982, and Tiff Wood had taken the bronze in 1983. That meant that there were two world-class scullers competing in Princeton this weekend. And the times of other scullers such as Bouscaren, Jim

Dietz and Brad Lewis were only a fraction off the times of these two.

Harry Parker, their coach, did not believe that concentrating the energy of all these talented young men into the single was necessarily a good thing. He wanted to direct some of these people to the double and quadruple sculls. In the double and the quad, the Europeans, who gave sculling a much higher priority, traditionally dominated. In both events teamwork and finesse were more important than sheer power, which worked against the Americans. In Europe young men in their late twenties and early thirties, often handsomely subsidized by the state, devoted long hours to honing their skills. In America, where rowing was subsidized only by parents, scullers usually dropped out in their midtwenties. A part of Parker, never expressed but fervently held, wanted the single-scull trials over. In his heart, he, too, tilted toward Wood, for Wood's rough style was better suited to the single, while Biglow's style would fit the team boats better. In America the team boats were usually patched together at the last minute, the oarsmen given three or four weeks to work out together and then sent to compete against the subsidized European teams, which had been rowing together for three or four, and sometimes seven or eight years.

Nonetheless, Parker, an intensely competitive man himself, was intrigued by the three-way competition he had been watching. He thought that all three of the scullers were so close in ability that there was no real favorite. Bouscaren, because of his size, might be a slight underdog. Both Wood and Biglow were strong enough to make mistakes in a race and still win. That was not true of Bouscaren. Only if he rowed an almost perfect race was he likely to win. Bouscaren amused Parker—Bouscaren competed at every level on every occasion, and the coach had been delighted that spring when a photographer from a national magazine had come by to take photos of the three oarsmen. Parker had watched Bouscaren jockey for position in the photos so that he would not be away from the center and would be as much a part of it as the others. The photographer had kept directing Bouscaren to stand toward one side, and Bouscaren had disregarded him, lest he be cropped out. He competes even at this, Parker had thought.

That Bouscaren competed at photo sessions did not surprise his friend Biglow. In 1981 they had been on the national team. When, at the end of the European tour, a photo had been taken, Bouscaren had stood next to Biglow. Biglow, the taller of the two, noticed that in the picture Bouscaren was standing on tiptoes and that at the very moment the photographer had snapped the shot, Joe had turned aside and was looking at Biglow's shoulder, trying to measure which one of them was taller.

CHAPTER
TWO

Tiff Wood, in order to compete on this weekend, had, as much as anything else, endured. He was five or six years older than most of his competitors. If in real life a generation lasted fifteen or twenty years, in rowing it was much briefer, perhaps only four years. The demands were so heavy, the alternatives so much more pleasurable that few stayed with it very long. Tiff Wood was now competing against young men who had entered college after he had graduated. His contemporaries, those men who had been a part of the same Harvard crew with him, watched his obsession with an odd mixture of admiration, envy and wariness. He had, they believed, been the least likely member of some great Harvard crews of the mid-1970s to stay with rowing. If he had been one of the strongest men on those Harvard boats, he had also been one of the roughest, an oarsman who responded to pressure and challenge by beating his oar even harder into the water and by giving more of himself. Surely, his contemporaries thought, Wood loved rowing, but they also thought he was proving something, too. On a legendary Harvard boat he had been relatively anonymous. Two of his teammates, Al Shealy and Dick Cashin, had become famous, at least famous by the standards of crew, and Shealy in particular had displayed an unusual gift for generating publicity. His boatmate Cashin felt that anywhere else and on any other boat Tiff Wood might have been a god, a god being the phrase that oarsmen used to describe someone who was a true star. But on that boat, his name had been known to few outside the inner world of rowing. Now he was competing for the right to be the dominant oarsman in America. In any real sense he had postponed his adult life.

There was, when he reached his midtwenties, something of a ritual to the manner in which he would get ready to quit rowing and then decide to stay on. He would call his father and say well, that was it, he had had enough, he was getting out. Then he would ponder the possibilities of the future and his own improvement, for he *was* getting better as a sculler, and he would decide to stay on. But for just one more year. In 1979, the vision of the 1980 Olympics had sustained him. In 1981 there had been the rise of John Biglow, a new challenge to deal with. By 1982, responding to Biglow, he had improved his technique dramatically. By 1983 he was rowing better than ever and suddenly the Olympics did not seem so distant. So he would call his father and say that well, yes, he was going to try it again. Just one more season. His father thought the Olympics loomed above all the other goals.

Tiff Wood had spent several years, and most particularly the past week, continuing to conquer all of the factors that threaten the individual in single sculling, above all the loneliness and the emptiness of working out alone at odd, cold and unpleasant hours. There were many moments when the impulse to quit was overwhelming. In team sports, the athletes were bonded by each other, and there was immense peer pressure to keep going. One dared not miss a practice for fear of letting his teammates down. Every time an athlete thought of getting back in bed in the morning he knew he would have to face the anger of his closest friends. But the sculler had to find motivation entirely within himself. No one else cared. The transition from sweep oarsman to sculler, was, Wood thought, largely a mental one; the difference in technique was negligible. He was fascinated by what his friend Charley Altekruse was going through. Altekruse had been a distinguished sweep oarsman at Harvard, and the physical adjustment to sculling was relatively easy for him. The handwork was more delicate, a hand on each oar instead of one oar manipulated by two hands. In addition, sculling demanded more pure strength than sweep rowing. But the mental adjustment had been much tougher. Altekruse hated to work out alone and had an almost pathological need for someone to share workouts with him. He was always calling Wood or one of the other scullers up to see if they could work out together, even if it only meant running up and down the stadium steps.

Wood knew what loneliness was like. The only pressure was the pressure from within. Harry Parker, the Olympic coach and his coach on and off for some fourteen years, was a flinty and unsentimental man. Tiff Wood knew that if he went to Parker one morning and told him that sculling was too much, that he no longer had the taste for it, there would be neither surprise nor disappointment on Parker's face. Parker would accept the decision without questioning it. He would probably not even ask Tiff if he was sure that he had made the right decision. Harry Parker accepted only those who were already motivated. That was a premise of rowing. He had no time for providing inspiration.

American scullers tended to be former sweep oarsmen—that is, they had rowed on an eight-oar shell using only one oar each. In college, rowing had been the overriding—indeed, obsessive—preoccupation for them. Upon graduation, uncertain of what they wanted to do professionally, they usually decided to stay with rowing a little longer. The choice became to find seven, three or one other oarsman to row with every day, or to row a single scull. Many of them became scullers. But after about three or four years, even the best went on to graduate school or to work on Wall Street.

Probably they were leaving sculling, Wood thought, just when they were getting better. His own body was much stronger now than it had been four or five years earlier (though the one thing he learned was that he needed more time to recuperate from all-out races than when he was younger). But the temptations of a normal life were strong, and it became harder every year to lead a life of such immense daily denial. Take his own training program, he said. The sky of predawn Boston during the winter months was not gray, it was black. There was a sense of acute loneliness sharpened by a wrenching cold. No sane person with an alternative to a better and easier life, a *privileged* life, was up and exercising at that hour.

"You have to force yourself to stay with rowing," Wood said. "If you put the first of the contact lenses in your eye, that is almost a sure guarantee that you won't go back to sleep. If you can get up and get past the bed, then you will reach the kitchen. If you can reach the kitchen, then you can reach the front door. If you reach the front door, you will reach the car, and if you reach the car, you can reach the boathouse. Each step leads to the next one. You keep pushing yourself so that you will not quit. You have to know when to listen to your body, because there is a part of you that always wants to quit and go back to sleep, and there is also a part of your body which on occasion is worn out and wants and needs rest, and then you have to listen." There were times when Wood hated his regimen, simply hated what he was doing and wanted desperately to be free. Yet he kept getting up and forcing himself to do what he thought he should do. Worst of all, in the winter the sheer pleasure of rowing was gone, the exhilaration of making so light a boat go fast was replaced by the painful and boring hours of work indoors. The speed was the pleasure for Wood. In an age of jet propulsion, the single scull might move only thirteen or fourteen miles an hour and weigh just under thirty pounds, but nonetheless it felt fast. Larger boats demanded *shared* strength; here he was all on his own. On the days when he rowed well, the pleasure was almost unimaginable.

In the nine years since he had graduated from college, he had held some quite good jobs, but there had never been any doubt that rowing came first. He had liked his job as an actuarial expert in Hartford after college, and Hartford, where the insurance man was king, was a wonderful city for that profession. But he had transferred to a consulting firm in Boston because Boston offered Harvard, the Charles River, some of the best rowing facilities in the world, other young men interested in the sport to compete against and Harry Parker. Wood liked the consulting firm; the people there had been very good to him, allowing him to adjust his work schedule to his rowing needs and even paying him half salary in those years when, preoccupied with rowing, he had showed up part time. Most of his college classmates were pursuing business careers in New York, which they saw as a faster track than Boston. That might well be true, and it was possible that Tiff Wood was jeopardizing his career, but New York was a terrible place in which to row singles.

CHAPTER
THREE

Tiff Wood had no illusion about why he was doing this. He was not doing it for his country. He was doing it for himself. If he won a medal, there might be an emotional moment on the platform when the anthem was played and personal and national goals merged. But that would be nothing more than the vindication of so much commitment and sacrifice. He exercised as many as 600 hours a year and practiced, hands on oars as many as 475 hours a year. Yet in a given year he might race only a few times, for perhaps a total of 130 minutes. Few sports had as great a disparity between the time committed in practice and time actually spent in game or race conditions. Given that ratio, how much this trial and the chance to row at the Olympics meant to the oarsmen competing became a great deal more understandable. Almost eight years of largely solitary effort was being summed up this weekend in a 7-minute race.

For in a nation where sports was big business, crew was apart. It had in no way benefited from the extraordinary growth of sports, both amateur and professional, which had been caused by the coming of television. By the 1980s, the marriage between sports and television (and merchandising) was virtually complete. Sports that the electronic eye favored underwent booms of astonishing dimension and became opportunities for celebrity and affluence. Sports that the camera did not favor atrophied by comparison. Many of the other great athletes who went to Los Angeles in 1984, the basketball players or the track and field stars, would have other chances to gain their moment of national recognition on the electronic eye during long and successful careers. Jimmy Carter would go on television again and again in his career. But the rowers would not.

Physically, rowing was remarkably resistant to the camera: Even if the television producers managed to rig a dolly on which the cameras could follow alongside the race, the angle of the camera might distort the finish, making a boat that was behind appear to be winning. Helicopters had been used with only marginal success. Worse, rowing at its best— the symmetry of powerful athletes pulling on their oars at precisely the right moment, in the grace of execution— seemed mechanical to the camera. When ABC covered rowing as part of an Olympiad, the network's haste to get away from this sport and on to something more telegenic was almost embarrassing. The camera liked power exhibited more openly, and the power of the oarsmen was exhibited in far too controlled a setting. Besides, the camera liked to focus on individuals, and except for the single scull, crew was a sport without faces.

That allowed it to remain an anomaly, an encapsulated nineteenth-century world in the hyped-up twentieth-century world of commercialized sports. Until television, sports had been largely divided between the worlds of the amateur and the professional. Even at the collegiate level, certain sports such as football and basketball became tinged with professionalism. But bastions of amateurism such as track and field were now beginning to fall. A top amateur track star named Carl Lewis, an immensely talented young man who might possibly win four gold medals in the summer Olympics, reportedly made $1 million a year in appearance fees and endorsements and was already a serious collector of antiques and crystal. When the Dallas Cowboys football team drafted Lewis as a possible wide receiver, Lewis's coach pointed out that they would have trouble signing him, not because Lewis did not want to play football but because their salary was likely to represent a considerable decline in income for Lewis. Some of the new affluence in track and field was a reflection of television's interest in it, although the networks put track on only when there was a vacuum in schedules or when, during Olympic years, there might be Soviets for these young (black) athletes to beat. Part of it as well was a reflection of a changing society: As America went from a blue-collar to a white-collar society and feared becoming sedentary, more people than ever before had taken up running and jogging, greatly increasing the possibility for endorsements and triggering the interest of Madison Avenue. That interest was great in ordinary years; in Olympic years, it was pervasive.

The turning point of Madison Avenue's heightened interest in the Olympics was the surprise victory in the 1980 winter Olympics of the U.S. hockey team over the Soviet Union. College hockey had never before fascinated the viewing public, but a victory over the *Russians* was another matter. Many of the commercials aired during the 1984 winter games reflected that triumph and Madison Avenue's expectations for another. The commercials portrayed clean-cut, farm-bred, young American kids bidding farewell to family, going to the hockey camp, giving it, as they say, their best shot and ending up with the magical gold. The commercials were so successful that myth and fact blended together as one. They helped convince a nation of decidedly less than great winter athletes that, in fact, it was going to win medals that were not in the cards. The embarrassment caused when the commercials exploiting the 1980 hockey team turned out to be better than the 1984 hockey team was palpable. The coach of the 1984 team said that for a time he felt almost ashamed to come home. Now Madison Avenue was shifting from hockey to the summer Olympics, using principally runners and pole vaulters instead of skaters. Some athletes, under the looser regulations governing amateurism, were huckstering products. There was one runner who liked something called Z-bec, and there was another runner who swore that his schedule was so busy that he had to eat Snickers, a candy bar that helped him make the Olympic grade. Marathon running, which once had been almost as arcane as rowing, now had stars who were getting rich from endorsing running shoes and breakfast cereals. But rowing remained old-fashioned, only in part because the $2,000 or $3,000 price of a scull was beyond the means of a mass public. In the world of the professional and the pseudoamateur, the sport of single-scull rowing, had, however involuntarily, remained a citadel of the true amateur.

That would have pleased Andrew Carnegie, for whom the lake where the trials would take place was named. Rich though he was, Carnegie was a serious believer in the physical and spiritual good that came from rowing. In 1903, Woodrow Wilson, then president of Princeton, had approached Carnegie hoping for a huge donation for a graduate college, the chief ornament of which would be a law school. The fund raising up until then had not gone particularly well. Wilson needed about $1 million and had fallen considerably short of it, though he had traveled around hitting up wealthy Princeton alumni. In a long letter to Carnegie asking for money he had pointed out that Princeton was American, and in his words, "thoroughly Scottish." Carnegie visited Princeton and told Wilson what his young men needed was not a law school but a lake to row on. In addition to being a sport that built character and would let the undergraduates relax after all that studying, rowing would keep them from playing football, a roughneck sport Carnegie absolutely detested. With that Carnegie gave $150,000 to dam a nearby stream, and Lake Carnegie was born, financed and named. Princeton never came up with a law school (later Wilson told Carnegie, "we asked for bread and you gave us cake"), and football remained a more popular sport on the campus than crew. But who was to say, some 80 years later in an America that was an increasingly litigious society, that Andrew Carnegie had made the wrong choice?

Oddly enough, the oarsmen had not always been anonymous. There had been a time in the late nineteenth century when rowing, particularly sculling, was a celebrated sport. The newspapers were filled with the accomplishments of professional scullers and the challenges they laid down to their adversaries. As many as thirty thousand people might gather for a championship match in the late 1870s, and the top scullers made as much as $15,000 a year in purses and even more under the table from bribes and payoffs. In a way it rivaled boxing in those days. Sculling had been a raffish sport, populated by what were known as sporting types, and the amount of betting had been unusually high. The oarsmen themselves had often been Irish immigrants or the sons of Irish immigrants, beginning their trek upward in American society. Given the heavy betting, it was not long before more and more outcomes became suspicious and the sport as a public and professional spectacle grew tainted.

By the beginning of this century, rowing was strictly an amateur domain, and a regatta was only a vaguely athletic event. If the weather was good, lots of young people gathered near a riverbank, drinking pleasantly and completely out of touch with what was happening a mile or two up the river, where the race was either about to start or perhaps even taking place. Very quickly the boats would flash by, and the crowd would briefly wonder which one had won before returning to their refreshments. They knew that rowing was first and foremost a participant's sport.

The people who were most fascinated by rowing almost always rowed. It was, said Al Shealy, the stroke of the Harvard crews on which Tiff Wood had rowed, "a hermetically sealed world." During their college years the oarsmen put in terribly long hours, often showing up at the boathouse at 6:00 A.M. for preclass practices. Both physically and psychologically, they were separated from their classmates. Events that

seemed earth-shattering to them—for example, who was demoted from the varsity to the junior varsity—went almost
unnoticed by the rest of the students. In many ways they
were like combat veterans coming back from a small, bitter
and distant war, able to talk only to other veterans. Who else
knew and cared of this distant land, of this terrible sacrifice
and of arcane moments of bravery and heroism? Fittingly
enough, when oarsmen got married, it often seemed that
they married young women who rowed, or sisters of their
teammates. The cast of characters at a wedding or at a boathouse was often indistinguishable.

Failing to get their deeds and names known to the world
of outsiders, they had become the custodians of their own
honor, their own record-book keepers. They remembered
with astonishing fidelity each race, who had beaten whom
by how many seconds, who had rowed at what beat, who
had rowed through whom (for that was the phrase that oarsmen used, rowing through someone else, one man finding
extra strength as another tired). If they lost a particular race,
they remembered each mitigating factor, heavier wind in
their lane than in the winner's, a poor rigging in the boat, a
particularly bad airplane trip that had cost them two days of
rest. Because their sport was one largely ignored by the traditional media, it was also to a remarkable degree a sport
enshrined in myth rather than reality. Because their deeds
were passed on by word of mouth rather than by book and
newspaper, the sport gained a mythic aura. Fifteen years
later, members of Harvard crews knew that during an
Olympic camp a normally stern and unbending Harry
Parker had knelt beside Fritz Hobbs, one of his favorite
oarsmen, when Hobbs had finished his ergometer test and
passed out. Harry, who never showed emotion or even sympathy for an athlete, was even said by some to have mopped
Fritz Hobbs's brow.

Every bit of knowledge about another racer was an advantage. The competitors at Princeton knew that Wood was

probably the strongest but also the roughest oar, that he rowed well into the wind; Bouscaren, who was smoother but not as strong, was better with a tail wind. Biglow was slow off the mark but strong at the end. Bouscaren was the quickest off the mark but did not finish as strongly as the others. Jim Dietz, a former champion now thirty-five and back for his last hurrah, could probably row one very good race, but it would be hard for him to row all out in both a semifinal and a final in back-to-back races. They competed furiously with each other and then went out to dinner together and talked about rowing. It was not surprising that they were bonded to each other. Who else, after all, knew how terrible and bleak a boathouse was in the dead of winter on an early morning, and who else knew the pain involved in each race?

It was in its way a very *macho* world. The egos were immense—they had to be for so demanding a sport. Men of lesser will and ambition simply did not stay around. The oarsmen were almost to a man highly individualistic and exceptionally compulsive. "A world of Type A personalities," said Al Shealy, one of the great Type A personalities himself. Loyalty and rivalry were most finely separated. Bonded though they might be to each other, there were ferocious undercurrents of rivalry among them. Because the rowing community was a closed one, its rivalries and jealousies were greatly magnified. The slight by one rower of another, real or imagined, took on immense significance, and tensions within a boathouse were often considerable. It was, Kiesling wrote in his memoir of rowing, "like a friendship between duelists," even on the same crew.

If the loyalties and rivalries were narrowly balanced, the loyalties almost always won out. One reason for that adhesion was the pain. It was a critical part of the bond. It was part of the oarsmen's unwritten code that one did not mention the pain. That was considered unseemly and, worse, it might magnify the pain and make it more threatening and more tangible. It was as if by not talking about it, the pain might become less important.

In his fine memoir of the sport, Steve Kiesling, who had rowed on very good Yale teams and a national team as well, had described in detail the pain involved in the sport. Some of his teammates felt that by doing this, Kiesling had shown that he was never able to cope with the pain. If he had been able to, their theory went, he would not have written about it. By contrast, the legendary figures of the boathouse were men who had passed out and who had somehow managed to keep rowing. When Tiff Wood had been at St. Paul's, he had grown up in the legend of a rower named Mad Dog Loggins. One day at practice, Mad Dog Loggins had been in a boat that was asked to give a power forty strokes at the end of a workout. (A power stroke is one in which the oarsman gives every bit of power he can; a power forty is forty all-out strokes.) Loggins had responded so vigorously that he had passed out at the end of the power forty. That was the stuff of myths, to pass out not just at the end of a race but after a power forty.

If that was a critical part of the community, then there were other reasons for the rivalries within the same community. On other sports teams, Tiff Wood thought, athletes were aware of their limitations and their differences. In football, the lineman, he noted, knew that he was different from the quarterback, and in basketball, the forward knew that he was different from the guard. Only the second-string quarterback secretly thought he should be the starting quarterback. But each oarsman did essentially the same thing and thought he was the best at it, some of them secretly, some of them not so secretly. This egocentrism, Wood said, was particularly true among the port-side oars, who even within the sport were notorious egoists.

Port-side egos were almost generic. On the first day of practice, the coach usually asked for volunteers who thought

they might stroke the boat—that is, sit in the first seat and
set the pace that the seven other oarsmen would follow.
Since all the most egocentric people thought they should be
strokes, and since the stroke was a port oar, the most egocentric oarsmen all stepped forward. That divided the team by
ego from the start. Wood himself was convinced that he
should have stroked his Harvard crew. He had been both
admiring and mildly resentful of Al Shealy, who had stroked
the crew brilliantly. Those Harvard crews that Shealy had
stroked had been uniquely successful. They had lost only one
dual meet, they had won at Henley and many thought them
the greatest Harvard crew of all time. But nine years after
they had rowed their last race, a part of Tiff Wood was still
resentful of Al Shealy—while a part of Al Shealy recognized
that resentment and was ready to prove in complete detail
why he, rather than Wood, should have stroked those boats.
Wood knew there was a certain madness in believing this,
but he believed it nonetheless. He was also aware that one
reason he had ended up in a single scull was that it was the
only way he could get to stroke a boat.

Probably the world of rowing was, to a great degree, ge-
netically preselected. In countries such as East Germany,
where sports fell under state control, authorities physiologically tested young rowers to see who should and who should
not be encouraged. In America, fortunately, selection was
less mechanical. Those who were good endurance athletes,
whose lungs were unusually good at extracting oxygen from
the air and whose tissues were replenished to a high degree
during a race, usually liked the sport and did well at it.
Those who were physiologically less suited never liked it, did
not perform well and soon drifted away. (Gregg Stone, who
had watched and rowed with Tiff Wood from the time they
were in prep school to the time they were both singles champions, had thought that at first it was simply Wood's competitive drive that had made him successful. Later, as Stone
learned more about the physiology of the sport, he was in-

clined to believe that Wood's triumphs were based on an intense competitive spirit combined with such a strong genetic base that Wood was able to waste immense amounts of energy with poor technique and still succeed.)

Those who dominated in sculling were, said Fritz Hagerman, an Ohio University professor who specialized in testing athletes, such remarkable physical specimens as to be, in his words, almost physiological freaks. Their great ability was their capacity to take in oxygen at an astonishing rate, thus releasing the food inside them as energy. If the normal person could take in three liters of oxygen per minute, then a world-class rower such as Wood or Biglow could take in six liters per minute. This oxygen intake was the key to their power and placed them way above other athletes. Baseball players might consume about three liters; professional basketball players, playing a stop-and-start sport, might consume four. Six was virtually off the chart. Only bikers and cross-country skiers were close—indeed, in proportion to their body size they might take in a little bit more oxygen than rowers—but bikers and cross-country skiers were much smaller, and on a pure sampling, the rowers took in more oxygen.

There are two ways for the body to produce energy, the aerobic and the anaerobic; the aerobic, by far the more efficient, is what sets rowers apart. The more oxygen that is available to the body, the more quickly the body can use its foodstuffs to produce energy. The energy thus produced is measured in kilocalories, one kilocalorie being necessary to raise one kilogram of water one degree Celsius. Someone brushing his teeth produces roughly one kilocalorie a minute; someone walking through a parking lot to a car uses about four to five; someone jogging at a slow pace produces about six to eight. A cross-country skier produces roughly thirty kilocalories per minute, but an Olympic-class rower produces thirty-six kilocalories a minute.

If oxygen is the key to aerobic energy, anaerobic energy comes into play when less and less oxygen becomes avail-

able—but anaerobic energy is only one nineteenth as efficient, and it produces as by-products lactic acids, which
cause immense pain. Thus at the end of a race, when a rower
inevitably finds his normal supply of energy depleted, it is
replaced by a source that is far less efficient and a good deal
more painful.

If Tiff Wood was the favorite for the single sculls, he did not
feel like a favorite, nor was he sure he wanted to be one. He
had, because of the harshness of the Cambridge winter,
spent perilously little time on the water and even less time in
racing, for it was one thing to practice and another thing to
race. Whatever edge he might have over his chief challenger,
Biglow, was negligible, and it was entirely possible that there
was no edge at all. Harry Parker had warned Wood that
being the favorite meant that everyone zeroed in on you. But
off a fine year in 1983 it had fallen his burden to be the target for everyone else, particularly Biglow.

From 1981 to 1983, the rivalry between Wood and Biglow
had been one of exceptional intensity, not unlike that between McEnroe and Connors, with Biglow having a slight
edge. Then in 1983 Biglow, suffering from a bad back, had
rowed poorly, and Wood had dominated the event, winning
not just the single-scull trial but also the bronze medal in the
world championship. (Friends of Biglow's were not sure that
his back was the only problem. They felt he might have been
suffering from being the favorite in exactly the way Parker
described to Wood.) But Biglow was now medically and
psychologically ready, and no one, no American at least,
could come from behind on him. In the world of rowing, his
closing sprints were legendary.

CHAPTER
FOUR

A photo of John Biglow published several years ago in the *Yale Daily News* was the most revealing image Steve Kiesling knew of his friend. The photo made Kiesling more than a little uneasy. It showed Biglow rowing alone in a single scull, not in a race, simply rowing against himself and his own standards, drawing on some last desperate source of energy to push himself a little harder, his face contorted in pain. The pain, thought Kiesling, was primal, something that even Steven Spielberg could not have created. Looking at the photo, Kiesling felt that rowing touched something deep and almost Conradian in Biglow, a dark place of almost total rage, hidden away most of the time but always wanting to get out. Biglow's high-school coach, Frank Cunningham, had a slightly different view. Cunningham, by and large, was wary of heightened expressions of pain on the faces of rowers. He thought that more often than not it was a gimmick used to impress coaches, that to the degree that oarsmen avoided showing pain they would avoid thinking of rowing as pain. If they thought of it as pain, the pain would increase. But Cunningham believed that Biglow's face showed something else. "With John it's all concentration, and the concentration is in his face. I like it—mouth open, lips drawn back. Breathing through his mouth. It's like"—

Cunningham paused for a moment to think of a simile—
"like a predatory animal about to pounce on some smaller
one."

Biglow himself was aware that he rowed with such intensity in part because portions of his emotional life were unre-
solved and rowing provided the almost perfect outlet for
them. He had once asked one of his fellow oarsmen, Brad
Lewis, why Lewis rowed, and Lewis had answered that he
was essentially very hostile and aggressive and this was the
only positive channel he knew for the aggression. An answer
that direct and blunt had surprised Biglow, and Lewis had
added, "You're the same way, John. You have a lot of hostility, too. But you just ritualize it better and hide it better
through rowing." Biglow had thought about it for a while
and decided that Lewis was probably right.

Biglow, thought Kiesling, was almost certainly the best Yale
oarsman of the modern generation and quite possibly, given
the advantages of modern training techniques and modern
body-building machinery, the greatest oarsman in Yale
history. Though he had come to Yale from a private day
school in Seattle instead of one of the great eastern prep
schools where rowing occupied a special niche, he was a
skilled, well-coached oar, and his style was memorable, lean
and powerful. He was able to pull more weight than men far
bigger and seemingly stronger than he, and he was willing to
punish himself to an uncommon degree to achieve his objectives. When he had arrived at Yale, that school, one of the
handful in America that took rowing seriously, had slipped
badly in its rowing program. It was being beaten regularly in
dual competitions and, even worse, being beaten annually in
its four-mile race against Harvard. A turnaround had begun
the year before Biglow had arrived, but he had certainly
played a central part in the renaissance of rowing at Yale,
and many of his contemporaries thought of him as a kind of
model for what an oarsman should be—powerful, relentless
and indefatigable. Feeling unsure of the challenge ahead

and the pain they would face in a given race, they had taken comfort from Biglow, who never seemed to be fazed. If they met his standards, they, too, would be strong.

Yet many of them had retained a certain ambivalence about Biglow as a person. He was simply too different. Even his political ideas were different. He cared about saving the whales, while some of his conservative teammates in retaliation talked about a campaign to nuke them. Lacking social grace, he did not know how to make others feel at ease. If anything, he seemed to take a perverse delight in making others feel uncomfortable. If he was going to experience a certain amount of culture shock, he was going to bestow a little on his teammates as well. At Yale, crew members were primarily eastern prep-school sophisticates. There were certain clothes you wore and certain clothes you never wore, certain things you said and certain things you never said. Biglow was western, albeit with certified eastern genes. By manner he seemed almost willfully a hick. He wore the wrong clothes and said the wrong things. He was constantly asking questions of Buzz Congram, the freshman coach. The prep-school oarsmen on the freshman crew found him difficult indeed. Some teammates nicknamed Biglow The Coach. Others had a phrase for him that was more description than nickname. Biglow, they said, was Nuts as a Bunny. It stuck to him.

Yale was always hard for him. It was a place where everyone seemed to be smarter, more facile and more verbal. When he was in the seventh grade in Seattle, his teachers had discovered that he had a serious reading disability. "You cannot believe," the teacher in charge had told his parents, "how hard reading is for him." He had been placed in a special reading class that had been almost as embarrassing as the disability itself; he had been, in his eyes, placed in a class for those who were slow. He had so hated the stigma that he had set out to finish the year-and-a-half course in just one year. The teacher, who was very sensitive to his needs, remembered that he would sometimes come to class exhausted by the pressure of trying to deal with his disability. Often, at the beginning of the class, she told his mother that John could not even talk, all he could do was utter a groan of pain. In spite of this, feeling immense parental pressure to succeed, he had received good grades. But reading and writing remained exceptionally difficult for him. In college he read only what he had to for courses, and he had almost no concept of what it was to read for pleasure. He would never, in Ivy League terms, test well, either in an admissions exam or in class. His handwriting, friends thought, was almost childlike. Writing a paper for class was a form of minor torture. (His Yale average at graduation was 2.9 on a scale of 4; the list of medical schools that turned him down was awesome; and for a long time it was a real cliff-hanger whether he would get into medical school or not.) It was not Biglow's intelligence that was at issue. His problem was in the expression of that intelligence.

His reading disability had deprived him of social confidence. Williams College, where he had wanted to go, turned him down; were he not a legacy at Yale, son and grandson of loyal Yale men, he might have been rejected there as well. He had arrived in New Haven shy and socially awkward, and in his early years he expressed himself largely through crew. It was the one outlet that gave him confidence. The coxswain of his freshman crew, Dan Goldberg, thought that Biglow was like a Thoroughbred horse, fine yet high-strung and nervous, skillful and brilliant at one thing and awkward and shy and unsophisticated in everything else.

Without crew, he would have been completely stranded. After his freshman year, he had returned to Seattle, and friends had asked how he liked Yale. "I liked the athletics there a lot," he answered. "But what about the college?" one friend persisted. "I didn't like it at all," he said. "It was very hard for me."

Biglow was not only hypersensitive to any slight, he also hated to fail in the eyes of others. There were times in his junior year, when Yale was preparing for its annual race against Harvard and he was the stroke, that he would come back so disheartened by a practice that he could not bear to eat breakfast with his teammates. He blamed himself for whatever went wrong, and he was sure the others blamed him as well. If one of them had said anything even mildly critical during the meal, he was sure he would have blown up.

As he had got older, he had worked harder than most young men at trying to come to some level of self-knowledge, carefully examining his behavior and his eruptions of temper. When he was at Yale and in the years since, he liked to get others to talk openly about why they rowed and what they really thought. Such soul searching did not endear him to many of his peers. Some were made uneasy by his attempt to understand their behavior (Biglow's encounter sessions, they called them); and others worried that if the answers were known, they might lose some of the athletic drive that had propelled them thus far. All of this added to his reputation of being different. What had happened, of course, was that he had taken his social awkwardness and turned it around for protection.

Though John Biglow was unusually candid with his peers in talking about himself, he kept his learning disability a secret while at college. Thus his friends could never entirely understand him, for a piece was always missing. The debate about him that had raged during his entire four years at Yale still continued: Was he a hick pretending to be a sophisticate, or was he a sophisticate pretending to be a hick? Was he an idiot or a genius? Some of his friends and coaches thought of him as a man-child, others as a kind of childman. He seemed sometimes completely without guile, and in the next moment, all guile. Tiff Wood once defined his manner as "artificial innocence." Part of him was as sweet and innocent as Holden Caulfield, but the part of him that was an athlete was a pure killer.

He was a Yale graduate on his way to Dartmouth Medical School, yet he did not seem like a young Ivy League prince.

If at times he appeared inarticulate and ill-informed, at certain moments he could become exceptionally articulate, making it abundantly clear that he paid attention to *everything* with an almost cold-blooded eye. Yet a moment later he would revert to being the innocent hick again, wanting to know everything, wanting to be helped.

Between his innocence—whether feigned or real—and his willingness to ask astonishingly personal questions of virtual strangers, he often came up with a great deal of information. By putting the burden of the conversation on the other person, Biglow often found out far more about others than he revealed about himself. He had a special talent for keeping others off balance, of asking embarrassing questions to which he already knew the answer, in order to watch the response.

His manner made the older Yale oarsmen wary of him. The superlative athlete was supposed to be the athlete-cool or the athlete-passionate. But who ever heard of athlete-hick or athlete-innocent? What frustrated some of his Yale teammates was their knowledge that with his ability, his looks and his background he could so easily be like the rest of them but for some odd reason he willed himself to be different.

Because he had been socially awkward as a boy, he had sought friendship through rowing; and when he defined what he loved most about rowing, his was an unusual description. When most oarsmen talked about their perfect moments in a boat, they referred not so much to winning a race but to the feel of the boat, all eight oars in the water together, the synchronization almost perfect. In moments like that, the boat seemed to lift right out of the water. Oarsmen called that the moment of *swing*. John Biglow loved that moment, too, but he spoke of it in an interesting manner. What he liked most about it, he said, was that it allowed you to *trust* the other men in the boat. A boat did not have swing unless everyone was putting out in exact measure, and because of that, and only because of that, there was the possibility of true trust among the oarsmen. That meant that as a young Yale oarsman he might well be seeking different rewards than most of his teammates were.

Even his style of rowing, influenced by the University of Washington crews, was different. To eastern eyes it appeared much rougher and included a small backsplash at the catch when he drove his oar. As a freshman, Biglow had had an argument with Ed Chandler about it. Chandler, who had rowed at Exeter, insisted that the backsplash was a sign the boat was being checked, its progress impeded. They took the argument to Congram. Chandler had rarely been so sure of anything. "Well, actually," said Congram, "John is right." Chandler was stunned. He walked down to the boathouse and saw some of his friends. "You won't believe this," he said, "but I've just lost an argument on technique to *Biglow*."

Soon the eastern oarsmen decided that he might have a good technique but that he wasn't really pulling hard. The tipoff on this, they decided, was that the puddles left by his oars were not particularly large. Mike Ives, another of the prep-school oarsmen, had looked at Biglow's smooth stroke and small puddles and had said, *"He's not pulling."* That meant his stroke was all finesse and no muscle. No wonder, then, his technique seemed so good. That contention had ended one day during the winter when the oarsmen measured their scores on the ergometer, a particularly cruel machine that simulated a race on the water; it tested strength and endurance, and it left even the biggest and strongest men gasping for breath when they got off it.

Because everyone knew everyone else's erg scores and measured a fellow rower by them, erg day was a day of judgment. Most of the oarsmen signed up as late as they could, so that the other scores would be posted by the time they took their turn. For men like Steve Kiesling and Eric Stevens, big and strong, who had never rowed before Yale, this was a wonderful day, for the erg allowed them to go out and bust a machine without worrying about technique. Each oarsman was to row for 10 minutes. Dan Goldberg, the freshman coxswain, was monitoring the machine, checking the scores so that Congram would have not just the final score but also the splits, what an oarsman did at each increment of time. Some of the other oarsmen asked him to goad them, to push them a little harder. Biglow wanted none of that. "I don't want you to say anything to me," he said, "except to give me my stroke rating every minute. Do not say anything else." All the other oarsmen had gone out as hard and as high as they could, and then predictably they had tailed off in the final minutes. Biglow did not go out hard, but he went out very smoothly. His splits were consistent, and with about half of the test done he was only a little behind the best scores. It was, thought Goldberg, the most methodical performance he had seen so far. Then Biglow's splits began to go up, higher and higher. This was his sprint, he was finishing strongly, and he had timed his energy to the scale of the test almost perfectly. His score was 10 percent higher than that of anyone else. It was an astonishing performance. While all the other top oarsmen had more or less collapsed over their machine at the end, Biglow had gotten up as quietly and calmly as he could and then casually walked away from the machine as if he had been doing nothing more strenuous than reading a newspaper. His scores had been so high, his lack of physical grief so remarkable that Goldberg and some of the other oarsmen immediately checked to see if the machine had been broken. Could this freshman of only modest rowing size (Biglow was six-three and weighed perhaps 185 pounds; a truly big oarsmen was closer to six-five and 215 pounds) have pulled these scores, which were not only higher than all the other freshman scores but also higher than the scores posted by the strongest men on the varsity?

But even the ergometer scores heightened the sense that something about him was not quite right. Anyone intelligent would in some manner or another manage to give more signs of distress. No brain, no pain, his detractors said of him with a certain cruelty, and he was very much aware of what they said. Soon stories spread that his board scores on the SAT admission tests had been unusually low. He became known as a machine. Joe Bouscaren, his friend and competitor, also called him a machine, but in a different sense. "He's an aerobic machine," Bouscaren had said. Biglow knew they were saying this about him, and in a way he resented it. He felt the pain; it was, however, something he had come to terms with, a requisite part of his attaining his goal in rowing.

In truth Biglow was a perfectionist about both himself and everyone around him. In his freshman year he could not stand to be near the six-four Kiesling. The aversion was not personal. It was simply that Kiesling had never rowed before and therefore, however powerful he might be, he was also crude and lacked finesse. In a sport so demanding of technique, this lack of skill enraged Biglow. If the people in the boat behind him were talking or not paying attention, he would turn and scream at them. Goldberg, the cox, would try to mediate between Biglow and the others. On the day of their freshman race against Harvard, there was an unusually strong wind. Just before the race was to begin, Biglow started whispering instructions to the others on how to deal with the rough water, seemingly unaware that everyone was already wound tight. Goldberg could sense the storm coming, and it came, "John," said Kiesling, "why don't you mind your own damned business and row your own damned race."

If many of the other oarsmen were governed by the culture of class, albeit a class that rowed, Biglow was governed by a profound sense of the ethics of crew. It was as if frustrated by the real world he sought in the world of crew a purer, more ethical universe. He and Goldberg had a tempestuous relationship; they irritated each other at first, and it took them a long time to become friends. Goldberg had been a boxer in high school in Iowa, and he was as new to the ethics of rowing as he was to the culture of class. He had heard that part of the job of a coxswain was to provoke and push the rowers. He had done that in the beginning, trying to push them at the end of the race by screaming at them, *"How much do you want it? How much do you want it?"* The former football players who were rowing for the first time liked these exhortations, which fitted the way their high-school coaches had pushed them. But Biglow hated them. "Don't ever say that to me again," he had told Goldberg. "It is never a question of that. Never." For Goldberg it was his first lesson in the code of oarsmen: Whatever else, if they were not doing well, it was not because they did not want something badly enough. The pain was such a given that all oarsmen who competed deserved never to be questioned.

There were many different parts of the code: Every race was as much a race against yourself as it was against opponents. Crew was always imperfect; no matter how good your crew, you were bound to lose, if not a race, then the ephemeral feeling of swing, when a boat was moving perfectly. Because currents, tides and winds made times largely meaningless, it was a sport in which records had no value. A runner might know that he had bettered the time of those who went before him. The oarsman in a boat that had won every race would always wonder if his boat was better than one that was comparably victorious six years earlier. The only clue that his boat was probably faster came from other sports, for swimmers and runners were systematically improving on the records set by their predecessors. But there was no empirical evidence. Therefore, humility became part of the code: You did not boast of what you would do or had done, nor did you embarrass a loser. Because your adversaries had subjected themselves to virtually the same regimen that you did, you respected them as much as you respected yourself. Biglow hated the moment in his sophomore year when Yale won the Eastern Sprints and some of the Yale rowers held up their fingers as if they were number one; he hated it even more a year later when some of the Yale sophomores had taunted the Harvard boat. "The sophomores are good," he said later of that race, "but they haven't learned the humility of crew yet."

Tony Johnson, the varsity coach, was, like Goldberg, struck by the intensity of Biglow's belief in the code. Winning was important, but competing at a high level was equally important. John's favorite race, Johnson sometimes thught, was not a race he had won but the Eastern Sprints in his freshman year. Yale had come in third in a race won by Penn and in which a half second separated the first three boats. In conversations with Johnson, Biglow was always coming back to what a great race it had been. Johnson was also struck by the fact that Biglow was exceptionally sensitive to any possible denigration of another crew. He hated to see people judged negatively because they had not rowed well. Once Biglow and Johnson had stood watching a regatta, and Johnson had made some idle comment about how badly one of the crews had rowed. Biglow had been offended and had challenged him immediately. "John," said Johnson, "I didn't say they were bad people. I simply said they rowed very poorly."

His daily manner belied the intensity of his drive to win. Most highly competitive athletes give off a tangible scent of their ego and drive; it is impossible to be around them without feeling their ambition or watching them stake out territory. By contrast, Biglow seemed more like a child of the counterculture seeking a little more nurturing than like a rival who would pay almost any price to win in a particularly demanding sport. His competitiveness, thought Kiesling, showed much more in defeat than in victory. In victory he was able to retain the mask of innocence; in defeat the passion was manifest. Once, during a particularly informal Yale practice, Kiesling and Biglow had been told to stroke competing boats. Kiesling, knowing his boat was not nearly as good as Biglow's, had cheated and sneaked off to a quick two-length head start. Biglow, to his surprise, had been enraged and had screamed a wild rush of obscenities at him and everyone in the boat. When, in 1983, Biglow had had trouble with his back, and Tiff Wood had captured the bronze in the world championships, someone had asked Biglow if he had been pleased that Tiff had done so well. After all, they were good friends, and Tiff had been a remarkably supportive rival. Biglow had answered with stunning candor: "No, I was jealous, jealous as hell."

He had always been an achiever, even as a little boy. "What can you tell me about John?" a fourth-grade teacher had once asked his mother at the start of a school year; and Nancy Biglow, after thinking very long and hard, had answered, "He wants to excel."

But if he wanted to excel, he also did not want to fail, and he carefully chose the battlefields upon which he allowed himself to compete. During their Yale years, Kiesling had taken a biology course. Midway through the year, he had a vague sense that Biglow was in the same course. Kiesling regularly sat in front in the class, and from time to time he thought he saw Biglow far in the back. But when he mentioned the course to Biglow, the latter said he wasn't taking the course, he was merely auditing it. That was hard to believe. People did not audit courses in biology. They audited courses in the history of art or modern American history, but not in something so technical as biology. Later, Kiesling became certain that Biglow was taking the course but was waiting to find out how well he would do before admitting it. His friends thought the period after Yale in which he was trying to get into medical school was the one in which he was most easy to like. His marks were not very good and, great sculler or no, most medical schools were subdued about his applications. For the first time since they had known him, the mighty Biglow was having trouble with something. With his human frailty showing, he allowed himself genuine intimacy with his friends. Previously, the responsibility of being the best, of not showing weakness, made him admirable if not always likable.

More than most of his contemporaries, John Biglow bore the burden of family and of tradition. The Biglows were a *family*. They gathered annually, they kept in touch and they were as much aware of their obligations as of their freedoms.

Biglows always did well. John Biglow might be from Seattle, but the Biglows by tradition were old-school Easterners. It was the kind of family in which the past was inextricably linked to the present. If Grandfather Biglow's son, Lucius Biglow, had moved to Washington after World War II, it was because both he and his young wife, Nancy, wanted to be spared some of the burden of that past.

John's grandfather, Lucius Horatio Biglow, had both rowed and played football at Yale until his mother, John's great-grandmother, had watched a Harvard-Yale race and had seen an oarsman pass out over his oar. Absolutely appalled, she had urged him to give up one of the sports, and he, to her vast relief, chose football, becoming captain of the '07 Yale team. He had long ago passed away, but his wife, Grandmother Biglow, was, in her own way, a keeper of the family flame. Biglows, she was quick to tell friends of John, were a special breed, and it was clear that she meant it. Biglow men did certain things, and they most assuredly did not do other things. They did well at school, they were Christian in their attitude, they went to church regularly, they attended Yale, they behaved like gentlemen and they took proper jobs. The list of things they did not do was equally stringent. They did not drink, they did not cry, they did not show their anger and they did not swear. Her house was filled with a vast variety of Biglow athletic memorabilia, some of it dating back to the beginning of the century. When Yale came perilously close to rejecting Luke Biglow, John's older brother, she vowed to take down Grandfather Biglow's Yale banner. Fortunately Luke got a delayed acceptance, and the banner was allowed to hang. Her son, Lucius Biglow, had not shared in nearly so much athletic glory as his father; he played football, but his only award had been for the best attitude on the team. Still, he had continued the family tradition. Like his father, he had been a member of Skull and Bones; and as achievement was constantly held out to him, he now held it out to his children. As his parents had sent him out the door with a little verse about school, he had sent his own children out with the same words. "Happy day," he said every morning. "all A's."

John Biglow had grown up in an uncommonly privileged Seattle household that blended some of the freedom of the West with the traditions and obligations of the East. Nancy Biglow might be able to keep a vast menagerie of animals at her house, chickens, ducks, even a turkey, but the East was there in terms of life-style, obligations and education. The children would go to Lakeside, the best country day school in the area, and they would take up, and predictably excel at, sports such as tennis, soccer and rowing. John Biglow rowed in his first single scull when he was about ten; and, through the tennis club they belong to, he had good coaching from the start. It was an interesting home, loving and sensitive, with immense amounts of care and energy allocated to the children. If anything, thought one friend, the Biglows were too perfectly tuned to their children, unwilling or unable to allow them to make their own mistakes, giving them more protection than they needed. They had imparted to John Biglow a belief that his needs would be always understood, a belief that turned out to be not always true.

The house was not without its tensions, which surfaced more often than not between John and his father. The differences were classically generational. John always believed that his father, burdened as he was by the demands of his own parents, pushed his children too hard in terms of success and achievement, that his love for them was connected to their ability to achieve. John exempted his mother from that judgment; but to him his father was a man consumed by the idea that Biglows be successful. A Biglow should go to the best schools, should succeed in athletics and then should join a company and become president of it. The Holden Caulfield part of John rebelled. (At Yale he had loved rowing but had hated the Harvard-Yale race because it meant old Blues coming up and telling him how much a victory would mean in terms of Yale's fund raising that year. He did not like the alumni talking about winning instead of about rowing.

Sometimes he wanted to tell them that if that was what the race meant to them, they could row it themselves. To him the race should be for those who rowed it, not for those who would then give more money to Yale.) As a little boy in school he had had constant disciplinary problems, challenging the authority of his teachers again and again. His mother believed his attitude was a result of the unrelenting pressure on him, that it was his form of rebelling against a world where a B was not good enough because Biglows always got A's.

Lucius Biglow would always deny that his love was attached to achievement, but then he would say something that would convince John that it was. When, for example, John had applied to medical school, he was aware of the limits of his grades. But his father had spoken immediately of Harvard and Yale medical schools, the best. To John Biglow that was just what he was trying to escape from, the idea that Biglows had to go to the best schools and advance to the highest levels. He did not think he could get in, he had told his father; and Lucius Biglow had responded that if John wanted anything badly enough, he could have it. That seemed a perfect reflection of an endless loving struggle, of generations and attitudes never entirely harmonized. In the end John Biglow thought that his father did love him, but he believed as well that his father's esteem rose and fell with his athletic performances. It was ironic, he thought, that his parents had moved to Seattle to escape the kind of pressure that was in the end more a part of his father than his father knew. That left John Biglow a conflicted young man, for that desire for achievement was something that he at once responded to powerfully—and resisted with equal power.

CHAPTER
FIVE

No one knew John's feelings better than Joe Bouscaren, who had been John's friend, teammate and competitor for six years. Bouscaren had spent considerable time with the Biglow family in Seattle. In the fall of 1982, when Bouscaren was in his last year of medical school at Cornell, he had been required to spend two or three months at a series of other medical schools. Since he was completely committed to the idea of Olympic rowing and since he planned to follow some form of sports medicine, he had made sure his stops were all at places with good rowing facilities. One of these places was the University of Washington in Seattle, where he had stayed with the Biglow family, enjoying that family's exceptional hospitality as so many other young oarsmen had before him. The senior Biglows had liked him, even though the sense of his rivalry with John made the friendship a little delicate.

He was, they decided, very competitive but absolutely charming. One morning Nancy Biglow was having breakfast with him and she asked Joe about his plans for rowing.

"I'd like very much to make the Olympic team," he said.

"In which boat, Joe?" she asked. There was a moment of silence. "The quad?" she continued.

"That would be fine," he said. Nancy Biglow felt that

something was being left unsaid. It couldn't be that he wanted the single scull. The single belonged to her John.

"The single?" she said, almost not believing her own voice.

He looked at her. His eyes were lovely and perfectly innocent. He was smiling in the nicest way, sitting in her house at her breakfast table eating the breakfast she cooked. "The single would be very nice," he said. He wanted her son's place at the Olympics. A world of beautiful young killers, she thought. It was the end of her innocence about rowers.

The generational war between John Biglow and his father had amused Bouscaren. When Lucius pushed his son toward the most prestigious medical schools, John took his revenge by constantly challenging his father on the latter's diet, urging him to use less salt and sugar. The irony for Bouscaren was that, Grandfather Biglow's achievements as a Yale football player notwithstanding, John was athletically the most successful Biglow in history. Either this had not dawned on him and the rest of his family, or it had dawned on but not yet liberated him.

If his staying with the Biglows strengthened Bouscaren's relationship with John, it also on occasion stretched it, for John, like his father, was so meticulous about everything that being his house guest was not easy. In addition, Bouscaren sometimes sensed a deft element of gamesmanship in John's actions, as if John were subtly suggesting by his behavior his implied superiority as a sculler. That began to gnaw on Bouscaren. From the way Biglow talked (or at least in the way in which Bouscaren *heard* Biglow talk), there was a considerable difference in their abilities. It was not that Biglow failed to praise Bouscaren's improvement but that he did it in a way almost calculated to annoy. "You're really doing well now, Joe," he would say, "you're really improving—you're the third-best sculler in the United States." With John there was no telling how deliberate this was, for he was capable of being a gentle and good man and a brilliant gamesman all at the same time. When, at a later date,

Biglow saw his friend Kiesling, who was trying for the Olympics in the pair sweeps, he was very pleasant, but at the end he said casually, "Just remember, Steve, you'll do as well as you've prepared for it." Since Kiesling, with a full-time job in New York a a magazine editor, had been able to prepare for the race only haphazardly, it was not the most gracious of sentiments.

By most standards, Bouscaren had an absolutely admirable body. He was six-three, lean and well-muscled. But he was not big-boned, not broad in the shoulders, where oarsmen get their power. Walking around the boathouse, he looked like an athlete from another sport, perhaps an exceptionally well-muscled tennis player who had walked over to meet a friend. As a sculler rowing against Biglow and Wood in the past two years, coming in more often than not third, he had assumed that his problem was his size. So in the year leading up to the Olympics he had worked hard to build up his body, to break through previous limits of strength and, above all, to prove that the mind, not the body, was the final arbiter of performance. Only that belief enabled him to work positively with the body he had been given. In the past it had posed something of a mental block; this year he had convinced himself that it did not matter, that he was as competitive an oarsman as if he were six-four and weighed 210 pounds.

Harry Parker thought Bouscaren was probably the most competitive of all the top scullers. Bouscaren competed at everything. If long-distance running was a critical part of the Yale rowing program, Joe Bouscaren, initially an ordinary runner, fashioned himself into a quality distance runner. When, after the 1981 sculling season, he and Biglow had decided to build themselves up in the weight room, he had wanted exact measurements of their improvement and had regularly measured both his and Biglow's muscles to see which sculler's was improving more. During the winter months, he and Tiff Wood had gone cross-country skiing several times together. Cross-country skiing was a sport Harry

Parker encouraged, for it built up athletic endurance. Because he was lighter than Wood, Bouscaren usually beat Wood. As far as Bouscaren was concerned, a victory over Tiff in cross-country skiing was a mental victory that carried over to rowing. He suspected that Wood felt the same way, too, and that there had been diminishing interest on his part in more skiing.

The name Bouscaren was French. Anthony Bouscaren, his father, was sixty-one years old and looked twenty years younger. He had gone to Yale, where his athletic career had been interrupted by World War II. He had been a Marine transport flier during the war, and he later taught political science at Le Moyne College in Syracuse. He was a strong figure in the eyes of his three sons, a serious Catholic, a deeply conservative man politically and an intensely competitive weekend athlete. He was by no means a Little League father, yet his drive and competitive zeal—he won his club's tennis championship in men's singles at the age of sixty-one—was directly transmitted to his sons. He faithfully, perhaps more faithfully than any other of the fathers, attended his sons' games and regattas, and his support for them was absolute. But he brought with him at all times the completeness of his standards. In 1981, when Joe Bouscaren had rowed in the single final for the first time and had done exceptionally well, coming in third, just nipped at the end by Tiff Wood, his father had greeted him after the race by saying, "Damn shame, Joe, damn shame." John Biglow, standing next to Bouscaren, had had an instant sense that the standards, however unconsciously, had been applied again and that it was important for Joe to do even better the next time.

His sons were made constantly aware that Bouscarens did not waste their gifts. The oldest of the three, Tony, had played lightweight football at Penn, and Mike, the middle brother, had been a great football player at Yale in the late 1960s, an All-Ivy League linebacker. Mike Bouscaren, even by the standards of the Ivy League, was not particularly big, six-one and 195 pounds, but he was a quick and almost violent tackler. Mike was eleven years older than Joe, and Mike's achievements were the focus of family life when Joe was approaching adolescence. Joe sensed his father's immense pride in Mike when he talked to friends; Joe had a sense as he grew older that his father was in some way living through Mike's athletic achievements. Those had been great Yale teams: Calvin Hill and Brian Dowling (who inspired Doonesbury, the comic strip) had played on them. The Bouscaren family had driven down to all the games, and hearing his brother introduced to the cheers of sixty thousand people in Yale Bowl had been heady stuff for a ten-year-old boy. What Mike had done *meant* something in that house, and the desire to emulate those achievements was an important part of Joe's boyhood. He was very much Mike's brother as a boy, he liked the sense of shared achievement and shared pride. But he was also, he knew later, in the shadow of his brother.

He had played football at prep school but had not enjoyed it. For a time tennis seemed likely to be his sport. When he entered Yale, he was about six-two and quite slim, the perfect build for a tennis player. But the illusion of tennis died quickly. He was at best a limited country-club player, and the people who would play for Yale had already been on the junior circuits. So finally he turned to crew. Early in the fall of his freshman year, his tennis career abruptly terminated, he had wandered over to the Yale boathouse and asked for help in learning how to row. Even then the intensity was exceptional. Tony Johnson, the Yale varsity coach, had a sense that this young man wanted to learn everything there was about rowing in the next ten or fifteen minutes so he could stop wasting time and get out on the water and *do* it.

Like Biglow, who arrived a year later, Bouscaren became a critical part of the group that helped regenerate Yale rowing. Old-time Yalies were inclined to blame the decline on the radicalization of the campus during the Vietnam War; but Harry Parker's Harvard crews had been magnificent in those same years, they had worn their hair long, identified themselves with antiwar protest groups, written their senior theses on black power and gone to the Olympics. Indeed, Parker had taken a special pride in the intensity of the political commitment of his athletes. Joe Bouscaren, so competitive himself, thought Yale rowing remarkably uncompetitive. The strength of Harvard's crews came from the constant challenge from the third- and second-boat heavies, which were almost as good as the varsity. At Yale the oarsmen appeared content to wait their turn. A sophomore was not supposed to drive a senior out of the varsity boat. We'll row, the varsity oarsmen seemed to be saying, we'll be genteel with each other and will not be abrasive. Bouscaren by those standards *was* abrasive. Years later, Tony Johnson remembered that in Bouscaren's sophomore year he had taken two crews out on the river. Since it was early in the season, he had asked the new sophomores to introduce themselves. Each had done so, the most modest kind of roll call, until it had been Bouscaren's turn and he had said, "I'm Joe Bouscaren, and I'm going to kick your ass."

What he loved about rowing was the knowledge that what he put into training he would always get back on the water. He did well from the start, he was a good student of the style and he quickly became a mechanically gifted oarsman. He had to be good mechanically, for unlike the others, he had nothing left over to waste. He became the stroke of the freshman heavyweight crew, a considerable achievement for someone who had never rowed before. He also began to build himself up. For the first time he had a sense he could become a varsity athlete at Yale, and that mattered. He loved rowing but hated the fact that as the smallest man on the 1978 and 1979 varsity his place was never as secure as it should have been. Though he had stroked the varsity as a sophomore, by his junior year, his size threatened to make him expendable. A lot of talented sophomores, Biglow and his classmates, were obviously going to row for the varsity, and Tony Johnson privately felt that someone a little bigger and stronger might replace Bouscaren in the first boat. That

winter Johnson had driven his oarsmen with a series of unusually grueling indoor exercises; Bouscaren had done them
along with all the others, but at the end, when the other
oarsmen were barely able to stand up, he had done an additional twenty minutes of jumping rope to add to his conditioning. He would not be displaced. He saved his seat. A
year later, the Yale boat was bigger and stronger than ever,
and Bouscaren and Biglow were the two smallest men in it.
Johnson, like most crew coaches, preferred his weight in the
middle and his lighter men at the ends, one stroking, one at
bow. For a time Bouscaren stroked. Then Johnson tried Biglow at stroke. Bouscaren took it very hard, and there was
some dissident muttering from him. Finally one of the other
oarsmen went to Johnson and said that something had to be
done about Joe, that his unhappiness was poisoning the atmosphere. Johnson called him aside and, with an implied
threat in his words, told him that his complaining had to
end. The muttering stopped. He didn't like it, but he had
still made the first boat.

He had graduated from Yale in 1979. While many of his
teammates had tried out for and made the national team
that year, he had pulled back from rowing. His new world
was medical school. He still cared about keeping in shape,
and he bought a machine that simulated cross-country skiing. But after a year away from rowing he was surprised how
much he missed it. He had thought of sculling. Mike Vespoli, who had replaced Buzz Congram as the freshman
coach at Yale and who knew how to motivate Bouscaren,
had stood with him once at the Eastern Sprints. When the
subject of sculling came up, Vespoli, who wanted Bouscaren to
try it, said, as casually as he could, "I don't think you can do
that, Joe. It's too hard, and you have to find too much within
yourself. I don't think you can push yourself hard enough."
It was, he knew, the perfect way of lighting a fire in Bouscaren. (Four years later, right after Biglow had beaten both
Bouscaren and Wood on the Easter Sunday race in Cambridge, Vespoli, still wanting to motivate Bouscaren, had

said to Biglow, in Bouscaren's presence, "John, how did it feel to row right through Joe? It must have felt really good.")

In the summer of 1980, Bouscaren, home from Cornell Medical School, had started working out in Syracuse with Scott Roop, a champion lightweight sculler. He and Roop went out together almost every day, and Roop would give Bouscaren quite generous leads and then row right through him. But Roop, who was training hard, pulled Bouscaren up to his level; the latter became more serious about the sport and about working on the Nautilus machines. His brother Mike thought that for Joe there was the appeal of a sport in which the athlete worked things out for himself and practiced by himself. To Mike, it fit the way his younger brother had grown up. Their mother had died of cancer at the age of forty-six when both older brothers were already out of the house, and Joe had become a single child living with a single parent. He had been forced to develop a sense of self-dependence that most people learn only much later in their lives. He was, Mike Bouscaren believed, accustomed to finding his sources of strength from within. Nothing could be better preparation for a sculler. When he returned to Cornell Medical School after that summer, he decided to keep up his sculling. He would drive to New Haven on the weekends, sleep in the deserted Yale boathouse and take out a scull for as many hours as he could, balancing the intense mental and psychological exertion of medical school with the physical exertion of rowing.

He came gradually to love-sculling. He had always wanted to stroke because the stroke stood apart in a boat. In sculling every quality oarsman stood apart. He was no longer the slim little bow oar who was carried by the heavier guys in the crew. By 1981, he was spending more and more time in Cambridge so he could work out with the other top scullers under the eye of Harry Parker. Bouscaren was intrigued by the contrast between his Yale coach, Tony Johnson, and Parker. Johnson, a gentler and more reachable man, pushed his oarsmen as hard as Parker did physically but not as hard mentally. With Tony, he thought, if you were putting out a genuine effort, there was almost always some kind of verbal reward. But with Harry, whatever you did was never enough. The question that seemed to hang in the atmosphere of the Harvard boathouse, unstated but always there, Bouscaren thought, was: Are you really tough enough for this? The Harvard environment, he decided, was a colder one. If he never became entirely accustomed to it, it did push him to reach for still higher levels of excellence. His brother Mike, whom he had once admired so much, now admired him. Joe, he thought, had maximized both his physical and his mental abilities to an uncommon degree, thus permitting himself to compete against much bigger, stronger, more naturally gifted men. He had managed that not just because he understood the sport and his own abilities so completely but also because he understood the concept of relativity in competition. Joe did not go into an event hoping to set a record or to dominate others. Rather he shrewdly assessed his own strengths and limits as well as those of his main competitors and adjusted his race plans accordingly. (Tiff Wood tended to confirm Mike Bouscaren's judgment. Wood liked to row against Biglow because Biglow's races were so consistent. But he did not like to race against Bouscaren because the latter rowed a different race each time). To Mike Bouscaren, his younger brother had become an athlete of almost unbelievable mental toughness. He had no business competing in this world, and yet he was competing at the highest level. In 1983 the quality of his rowing had begun steadily improving, and there was a marked improvement in his endurance. In the last year Bouscaren had won three important races in which endurance was critical, the Head of the Schuylkill (2.75 miles), the Head of the Connecticut (3.5 miles) and the most prestigious of them, the Head of the Charles (three miles), where he had, to his absolute delight, edged out Tiff Wood. By all rights he should have been preparing himself for a team boat where his technical skill was badly needed. But he wanted to be the single sculler, and he was sure he was peaking just in time for the Olympics. In the early spring Mike Vespoli, who was helping the rowing association by checking on the sculling program, had called Bouscaren to find out how things were going. "Is there anything we could be doing that would make things better?" Vespoli asked.

"Well, there could be a lot more work on the quad," Bouscaren answered. The year before, he had rowed on the national quad, which had taken seventh in the world. Rowing with him had been Charley Altekruse, Bill Purdy and Biglow. There was the possibility that with more experience it might become a more competitive boat.

"Oh," said Vespoli, knowing exactly what he was doing, "are you willing to give up the single and row in the quad?"

"Absolutely not," said Bouscaren.

CHAPTER
SIX

As Tiff Wood walked among the other young businessmen in Boston, he appeared to be just another modest young man in Ivy League clothes, the actuarial expert with a consulting firm that he in fact was. Despite his six-one height and his 185 pounds, he did not look tall and powerful as one might imagine a great oar. In his street clothes, he seemed almost slight of build. But there was no fat on him, he was all muscle. If the normal human body fat was somewhere around 18 percent, his level of fat varied between 7 and 8.5 percent (skater Eric Heiden's was 7 percent). Only in his rowing clothes did the power in his body show his enormously strong arms and his immensely thick and awesomely muscled legs. The power in them was unmistakable; and when John Biglow spoke of Tiff Wood and his ability, he spoke first of his legs. Tiff Wood, in classic terms of muscularity, was much stronger than John Biglow.

In addition to his strength, Wood had an exceptional capacity to bear pain. Rowing, particularly single sculling, inflicts on the individual in every race a level of pain associated with few other sports. There was certainly pain in football during a head-on collision, pain in other sports on the occasion of a serious injury. That was more the threat of pain; in rowing there was the absolute guarantee of it every time. Pain in championship single-scull rowing is a given. Each race is like a sprint. But unlike a sprint, which usually lasts 10 or 20 or 45 seconds, a two-thousand-meter sculling championship lasts 7 minutes and is roughly the length of a two-mile run. The body quickly burns out its normal supplies of oxygen and then demands more. But less and less oxygen is available. That means the body is still producing high levels of energy, but it is making the sculler pay for it by producing a great deal of lactic acid as well. With the lactic acid comes greater and greater pain. In addition, the scullers are unable to pace themselves, as long-distance runners can. They might try to hold back a little bit of energy so they will not burn out at the end, but in truth they go all out from the very beginning. It is an advantage to lead in a sculling race; the leader can see the other boats behind him and does not get caught in their wash.

When a race was over and Tiff Wood had rowed at his peak, it took almost five days before his body was physically replenished. When he thought of rowing, the first thing that came to mind was pain. After the first twenty-five strokes of a race, his body ached. His lungs and his legs seemed to scream at him to stop. On occasion the temptation was almost irresistible. The ability to resist the impulse, to keep going in spite of it, to reach through it and summon extra resources of power while others, stronger and smoother of technique, were fading, made him a champion. But he could not think of racing without thinking of the pain. It was hard for him in advance of a race to sit and plan out what he intended to do because the very thought of racing filled him with dread of the pain.

But he was also aware that his ability to absorb that pain had made him an exceptional competitor. He had rationalized all of it very carefully, going over and over in his mind the pluses and minuses of what he was doing. The race itself was a terrible ordeal. The pain bordered, he thought, on a kind of torture. The worst part of the torture was that it was self-imposed. There was no need to go through with it. But he had willed himself to deal with it; he wanted to measure himself against the best, and the only way to do that was to bear the pain.

In truth, deep down, he liked this aspect of the sport because it permitted ordinary and not particularly talented young men and women to reach beyond themselves. "I think," he once said, "that what I like about it is the chance to be a hero. Every day in what seems like a very ordinary setting there are heroes in every boat, people reaching down to come up with that much more energy to make it work. I like that, I honor it and I think that is special in this world." In the end, rowing made him feel good about himself.

Parker, his coach and a former Olympic sculler himself, thought that Tiff Wood was particularly good at calibrating exactly how much energy he had left and giving every single bit. Part of his strength, Parker thought, was in coming across a finish line on the surge of his last possible stroke, absolutely depleted. This was true even in practice, and Parker recently had a graphic illustration of it. He had, near the end of a long and punishing workout, asked Wood for a final twenty power strokes, and Wood had given them. But Parker had not been paying attention, and he had asked Wood for ten more, ten more strokes from a body that was finished; and Wood, the most modest and proper young man imaginable, had screamed at Parker in a kind of elemental rage, "Fuck you!"

Early in Wood's college career Parker had decided that any attempt to make him row with greater finesse would be counterproductive. He was impatient with technique. The best way to coach him, Parker decided, was not to coach him but to leave him to his furies. What set Wood apart was will, the power of the mind to bend the body to its uses. There was a certain madness to that, Wood knew, but there was also a purpose. He had, after all, been raised in a tradition in which sacrifice, if not pain, was an essential ingredient. He believed, he said, in the Puritan ethic, not the leisure society. A world where people sought only leisure seemed empty to him. The best thing about rowing was in the obstacles it presented, even if these were, in his words, manufactured obstacles.

He was, of course, intensely competitive. Rowing indoors on the tanks during the long, boring winter months, he invented competitive games to keep him going—he would try to row a larger puddle than the oarsman just ahead of him. (He was scrupulous about not cheating, though of course the other oarsman did not know the contest was going on.) When Wood graduated from college he had gloried in taking the tests for both business and law school and had done exceptionally well. He always tested well. Some friends had teased him about the fact that he should have taken the tests for medical school as well. Just one more group of applicants to compete against, they said.

His fiancé, Kristy Aserlind, also a rower, liked going for long, aimless walks. Tiff Wood did not. If Tiff went for a walk, there had to be a form to it, 3½ times around the block. It would be even better if there were an existing record for those 3½ blocks that he could compete against.

There had to be form and purpose to the walk because there had to be form and purpose to life. That was one of the interesting things about rowing. Those who competed at this level did so with a demonic passion. Yet there was no overt financial reward at the end, nor indeed was there even any covert financial reward, a brokerage house wanting and giving special privilege to the famed amateur. Yet the athletes were almost always the children of the upper middle class, privileged, affluent, a group that in this society did not readily seek hardship. One could understand the son of a ghetto family playing in the school yard for six hours a day hoping that basketball was a ticket out of the slum; it was harder to understand the son of Beacon Hill spending so much time and subjecting himself to so much pain to attain an honor that no one else even understood. Perhaps in our society the true madness in the search for excellence is left for the amateur.

For Tiff Wood was a son of Beacon Hill, the home of the American establishment, and he had gone to the best schools, as had his father before him. The Woods were not very old Boston. Reginald Wood, the grandfather, who had quit school at fourteen to be a runner on the floor in Wall Street, had been successful in the stock market. Very much a self-made man, he had been determined that his children would have the best in education.

Richard Wood, Tiff's father, had gone to Harvard, and in his early sixties, he was as lean as his son. He still ran three or four miles a day, and on weekends he usually ran ten miles a day. In his late fifties, he had run in three marathons. In the first one he quit after seventeen miles. In the second, when he made twenty-three miles and could no longer run, he alternately walked a block and ran a block, finishing in 5½ hours. The next year, better prepared, he made it home without limping, in 4½ hours. He loved the outdoors, and he was the first one on the ski slopes in the morning, the last one off in the evening. He took a special pleasure in being on the slopes on days when it was ten degrees below zero and no one else would go out except, from the time he was eight years old, his son Tiff. There had never been a doubt in Richard Wood's mind that the boy was determined to stay with his father on all occasions, to push himself as hard as he could even if he had to absorb an unusual amount of punishment in the process. If he was not competing with a father (for the question of whether an eight- or nine-year-old competes with a parent is a difficult one to answer), he was certainly proving something to his father, again and again. Even as a little boy he had been obsessive. In kindergarten, he had become so voracious a reader that the school at the end of the year had given him a handsomely lettered certificate proclaiming him "the World's Greatest Reader." His father thought his willingness to take on excessively harsh challenges bordered on a form of masochism.

When he was ten, he had stayed at the home of a friend named David Hansen and they had decided to sleep outside in the simplest kind of tent. It was early spring and cold. That night there was a horrendous rainstorm. In the middle of the storm David Hansen had come inside, but the next morning Richard Wood was appalled to find his son asleep in four inches of water. From then on he had realized that his son was always going to push himself to the limits in terms of physical risk, that he was not just proving something but gaining recognition as well.

A year later they had gone mountain climbing in New Hampshire, and very high up they had come to a tiny pool of water that was at most twenty feet in diameter. The water was absolutely ice cold. Above it stood a very steep mountain cliff, perhaps thirty feet high. Anyone diving from it to the pool would have to make an almost perfect dive or be splattered on the rocks. Richard Wood had taken one look at the cliff and known exactly what was going to happen. Tiff was going to want to dive in, but the pool was so small that he could easily miss it. "It'd really be something to dive in from there," Tiff had said. "I think I'll pass," Richard Wood had said. He had watched as Tiff had measured the distance and he thought, Do I tell him not to do it? He had decided, no, he could not forbid him, and Tiff had made one dive and done it cleanly, a dive into water that no one in his right mind would want to swim in in the first place.

Those were not particularly happy years for Tiff Wood. His parents' marriage was coming apart and they were about to get a divorce. He found himself painfully shy, and his feelings about things were completely internalized: It was not that he was without feelings, it was that he found no way to express them. Just after his parents had been divorced, he had once started to cry over some minor incident. When his stepmother had tried to comfort him, he had turned away from her abruptly. "I don't want anyone to feel sorry for me," he had said. Given a chance by his father to stay at home or go away to boarding school, he had seized the chance to go away.

He had arrived at St. Paul's School in 1967, thirteen years

old, small for his age, unsure of himself, confused. He was, he realized later, a very shy little boy who kept all of his pain inside. At St. Paul's he had not done well in the beginning. He was smart, but he had realized immediately that too strenuous a use of his intelligence and the accumulation of exceptional grades did not bring popularity. He was rebellious and wore his hair long. Popularity eluded him. "The people I wanted to be my friends were not interested in being my friends," he said of that time. "I thought they were making a mistake. But it was not easy to show this to them."

At St. Paul's popularity and status were in some indefinable way tied to things that might well be outside his reach, such as looks and size and athletic accomplishment. He had never been a particularly gifted athlete. His eyesight was terrible, and in those days there were no soft contact lenses. He felt clumsy and awkward at almost everything, and then he tried rowing. On the first two days he had gone out, the conditions had been appalling, cold and snowy. The boat had been filled with water and he had loved it. The harsh weather, which drove off most of his contemporaries, drew him in. He had always felt comfortable in such weather. From the start he had had a sense that this was a sport in which he could excel, for it required only strength and dedication, not skill or grace or timing.

At St. Paul's, rowing had a particular prestige, it was bound into the tradition of the school as much as football was. Besides, football was out. He could barely see the ball. But in rowing the athletes looked behind them. His mother, aware of his problem, encouraged him in crew; his father still preferred football. Tiff Wood's instincts told him crew was his sport. Whatever price was required to succeed in rowing, he decided he would pay it. He had been rowing what were called club boats, which were like intramural boats, and had noticed that the coach of the crew, Richard Davis, was very popular with the more senior rowers. Davis was young, just out of the Air Force, and at night he ate with the students;

Tiff Wood by chance had been assigned to his dinner table, and Tiff quietly sat there night after night, absorbing as much of this cherished atmosphere as he could. He sat there torn between desperately wanting to be noticed and just as desperately wanting not to be noticed. He was aware that he was almost too small to be in the company of such important and accomplished young men. He was so silent that he was not even sure that Davis had noticed him.

In his second year at St. Paul's another boy broke his collarbone, and Davis had reached down and placed Wood in the third varsity boat. After that his life centered on rowing. He was awkward at everything else, but about this he felt strong and confident. It was his one chance of asserting himself. If almost everyone else had better technique, Tiff Wood would compensate for lack of finesse by simple determination and will. His instinct, when something went wrong, was simply to pull harder, to punish himself a little more. That became his trademark. Richard Davis was the perfect coach for a young man like him. Davis had coached for a time at Harvard while a graduate student, and he patterned himself after Harry Parker. Davis was less interested in technique than in conditioning and attitude. If his rowers were in better shape and had worked harder, he taught them, they would win. "You have to row until it hurts," he told them. That was perfect for Tiff Wood. The key was not God-given, it was in the rowers themselves. If, at the end of a grueling afternoon on the water, Davis called for a run back to the school, which was a mile away, there were perceptible groans from the other kids; but Tiff Wood would lead the run back with pleasure showing on his face, for this was his territory, these were his rules.

Soon he began to build a reputation as a very strong oar. On some days he thought he was rowing so well that he could move a boat all by himself. If he pushed himself to his absolute outer limit, pushed the level of pain above any acceptable limit, he could make his boat win. Knowing this, he punished himself that much more. His mother faithfully came to all his races. "I'll see you at Henley one day, Tiff," she said.

The next year he returned to St. Paul's and was assigned a new dorm. As he approached the form on the first day, he saw one of the most admired boys in the hip, irreverent crowd he hoped to join, one of those golden boys for whom everything seemed to come easily and who had seemed a thousand social levels above him in the past. "Hello, Tiff," the boy had said. Tiff had arrived. If, in years to come, he stayed with rowing much longer than any of his contemporaries, it was partly out of gratitude and partly because rowing was so crucial to him. At a time when he was most vulnerable, rowing had given form to his life and brought him confidence.

He was not a pretty rower—indeed, he was rough and elemental. "I am," he said, "propelled by a sense of urgency." His nickname, befitting his style, was The Hammer. That was a term, slightly pejorative, for a rower who used brute strength to cover up technical deficiency. He was the quintessential hammer. Because he had a knack for moving boats—his boats *won*—his coaches both in prep school and college had been reluctant to tamper with his style and add technique. It was as if he were too impatient to use his power to bother to learn technique, for in the transition to greater finesse, at least at the start, power would have to be sacrificed. When he drove his oars into the water, he did it with such fury and strength that it virtually drove a physical shock into his body. He was rough at the catch, the moment when the oar hits the water; he knew that, but he was forgiven even that flaw. When his boat was behind, his response was always to punish himself a little more. "Which one is Tiff?" his stepmother, Jane Wood, quite new to the sport, had once cried while watching a Harvard boat race. "I can't pick him out." "He's the one who keeps moving his head," answered one of her friends, more sophisticated about rowing.

Some traditional scullers were offended by the crudeness of his technique. For a long time this did not bother him. If anything, he disdained those who placed a premium on form. "Form is for gynmastics and figure skating and diving, not rowing. I want to win. Rowing is about winning. If you win, then everyone says your form is good anyway," he once said. He was quick to summon historical precedents for the defeat of finesse crews by strong but crude crews. He took pleasure in talking about a famed (and victorious) University of Washington crew that was so rough it was known in the sport as "Lurch, Wobble and Gobble." He liked to quote Steven Fairbairn, an Austrailian oarsman who had been a critic of the traditional view of rowing that style was more important than power and endurance. "Drive at your blade," Fairbairn had said, "and let your body and slide take care of themselves." Tiff Wood took solace in those words.

CHAPTER
SEVEN

He had never thought of going anywhere else but to a rowing school, Harvard if possible, for Harvard in the 1960s and the 1970s was the great center of collegiate rowing. In his freshmen year he had weighed about 165 pounds, and he had tried for the lightweight crew. But he soon switched to the heavies for two reasons: first because, as an oarsman, he had to sacrifice enough in his life and he did not want to starve himself constantly to make the weight for the lights; and second because, in the world of rowing, true status and prestige belonged to the heavies. The lights were merely the opening act in most regattas. His career at Harvard was a distinguished albeit somewhat anonymous one. In 1972, he rowed on a great and undefeated Harvard freshman crew that had gone on to Henley and won the Thames Cup. In 1974 and 1975, his junior and senior years, respectively, he had rowed on Harvard crews that never lost a race in domestic competition. Those crews were very good and very cocky.

The stroke was Al Shealy, with his flair for publicity and self-promotion that was almost unparalleled in Harvard rowing history. Journalists wrote about him. Nonrowers knew his name; and if he was not a natural eccentric, then he was a brilliantly self-made one, on occasion setting off minor bombs in his own room to frighten his roommates. As Harvard won race after race, Shealy began to put his signature on each victory. When Harvard made its move and went by Yale or Penn, he would shout out—it was unheard of in the gentlemanly sport of rowing—"Good-bye, Yalies!" or "Farewell, Quakers!" Sometimes it was simply, "So long, suckers!" Other crews hated Shealy and the Harvards; it was bad enough to row against them and be beaten every time, but his cockiness made it all the worse.

A race with the University of Washington had highlighted the Harvard crew's elitism. Since most of Harvard's victories were against *eastern* crews, the Washington oarsmen regarded the race as one for the national championship. In the eyes of the Harvard oarsmen, a race on that same trip against Wisconsin, a race they had barely won, had already given them the national title. Before the race, to be held in Seattle, Shealy had played his usual gamesmanship by announcing plans for a naked heliborne raid on the Seattle Space Needle. The Washington oarsmen were duly offended by the Shealyisms ("I think that they probably saw us as a bunch of extremely arrogant upper-class prep-school-Harvard kids, and I think they were probably right," Shealy said years later.) The Washington oarsmen had their own means of retaliation. Timing was critical. At the exact moment that the Harvard crew arrived at the boathouse, the Washington oarsmen were getting ready to row. They were immense, obviously the biggest crew in the country. They all wore dark glasses, they had all shaved their heads, and they were stripped to the waist and oiling their bodies. They were at the least fifteen pounds a man heavier. But it was more than that, Shealy thought, they were *ominous*, so big and muscular, "like genetic defects, with these huge, bulbous muscles. Like primitive man. We were these skinny, snotty, little eastern kids." Harvard won by two lengths. With a third of the race left and Harvard pulling ahead, Shealy had yelled, "Farewell, Huskies!"

Harry Parker watched Shealy's antics with a certain mild

ambivalence. If they represented unnecessary arrogance, then nonetheless it was arrogance earned. His crew behaved as if they were that good because they *were* that good. They became known in rowing history as "the Rude and Smooth" Harvard crew. The name came from an early victory when an older rowing aficionado had come up to them after the race and had told them that they had rowed a very smooth race but their antics were very rude. They loved it. They immediately became Rude and Smooth. There was madness in what they did. But then, why not? "Physical madness—and surely what we were doing every day, putting so much into so little was a form of madness—begets cultural madness. We were culturally mad," Shealy said. Because Shealy was a World War II buff, they practiced in World War II helmets. Because Shealy was a Patton freak, they called their boat the *George S. Patton.* Before races Shealy liked to quote one of Patton's most famous World War II speeches, about going through the Huns like shit through a goose, taking particular pleasure in doing it in the same boathouse as the East Germans. The Harvard crew began to have rituals. Before a race with Yale, desperately hungry at night because of the caloric output of their training and anxious to get out of the training camp, they would make what were called doughnut runs. Into the Jack-in-the-Box they would drive, and Tiff Wood would grab the microphone that customers used to order. "We want five hams," he would say, and the man on the other end would say that they did not serve ham. "Yes, you do—five hams coming up," Wood said, and then they would moon.

They were very good. Four of them, every port oar, eventually made the national team, and two of them, Wood and Gregg Stone, became national champion scullers. They not only won, they won by a lot. They began to call some of their victories "horizon jobs" because there was so much daylight between them and the next crew. They were not without tension. Tiff Wood's belief that he should have stroked those crews was a small but very real barrier in terms of friendship between him and Shealy. Gregg Stone did not always row in the first boat; this was a source of some annoyance to him, although there were others who thought Stone tended to coach too much. The competitiveness showed in their daily workouts when they tried to beat each other. In running stadiums (a Harry Parker off-season special, the *tour de stade* it was called, running up and down each of the thirty-seven sections of the Harvard stadium), they kept times, and records were posted. Gluttons did two tours, but that was not required. Finishing in under 25 minutes was generally considered good. Worse than the *tour de stade* were the sprints, which were done in relays, from the stadium floor to the top and back, five repetitions of five sprints. They competed on the ergometer, though Dick Cashin, the six man, was the strongest, with scores of about 3,800 for 6 minutes while everyone else hovered closer to 3,600. They competed in the weight room as well, but no one was particularly good on the weights; that was a sign of being musclebound, they thought, and they wanted flex in their power, not stiffness.

Part of the fierceness of their internal competition came from the fact that it was so hard to hold a seat in the boat; the junior varsity and the third boat were loaded with people just as intense and committed. In the way they drove each other, they were an extension of Harry Parker. The intensity showed in the seat racing. Seat reacing was a primitive form of trying to find out who really moved a boat. It was fiendishly simple and brutal: Two oarsmen were pitted against each other in competing eights; after an all-out race, they switched boats. Gradually, over the weeks of practice, the coach could tell who was regularly winning and who was regularly losing and pick his boat accordingly. Tiff Wood was a violent seat racer. "He was absolutely savage," Cashin, his much bigger teammate, remembered. "I don't think he *ever* lost a seat race. I was bigger and stronger and I was better on the erg and I made the national team in my sophomore year, which was unusual, but I could never beat Tiff in seat racing. I came back from being on the national team in my sophomore year and I had a hard time getting a seat because Wood was there. I once tied with him in a seat race—it was on April seventeenth, 1975; I remember it because it was my birthday. But I never beat him."

Harry Parker tended to hold Shealy back from seat races; Shealy was a great stroke, skillful and deft and a compelling figure. Part of his strength was his bravado. It was critical to his psyche that he consider himself the preeminent oarsman of the group. It would not do if he lost in intramural competition to others in the boat. One year the Cal coach had said, "We'll never beat Harvard as long as Shealy and Cashin are there." The remark had stung everyone else, particularly Tiff Wood. Gregg Stone was sure that one of the main reasons both he and Wood had gone over to sculling was to prove that they had been as much a part of those boats and those victories as Shealy and Cashin had; and they were proving it, in Stone's words, "to Shealy and Cashin, to Harry Parker and even to our parents. My father, who used to row, would come down to see Shealy and Cashin race—even he caught the hype and, God, that irked me. Five years later we were pushing ourselves as national-champion scullers to prove that we were as much a part of those eights as they were."

There had been a certain wildness to Wood at prep school. He did drugs, mostly pot, and a little psychedelic exploring. His crowd was a hip one, not a jock one. At Harvard he was still passionate about rowing and still wild. The other oarsmen roomed together, but Wood for most of his years was with a different group, longer hair, more drugs, different interests. The drugs soon faded out of his life, replaced by a growing commitment to rowing. Looking back on it, he saw the drugs as part of the times, a way of rebelling within entirely comfortable limits. He was an immensely talented student, but he was on probation twice and missed one season of rowing because of poor grades. He was on probation because he simply had not gone to a particular class all year. His long, leather trench coat and dark glasses further stamped him as a leftover child of the 1960s in the mid-1970s. He liked the schizophrenia of his images. If, to most outsiders at Harvard, crew was the most inside or clubby of sports, then he was both an insider and an outsider.

The savagery with which he rowed bordered on a kind of athletic violence. His reputation among the other oarsmen was that he was a powerful oar but on occasion an erratic one. There would be moments, even his friends thought, when he would try to do it all, try to move the boat entirely by himself, and that always hurt the boat. In their freshman year there had been a heat at Henley, an early one with more to come. They had been under orders to get a three-quarter-length lead and hold it and thus conserve strength for the races still ahead. But midway in the race there had been Wood, enraged by his inability to turn on full power, screaming at his teammates, *"Let's go! Let's go! Let's go!"* Even as he was screaming, Ted Washburn, the Harvard freshman coach, was bicycling on the bike path along the river, and he could clearly hear Wood. *"Confidence, Tiff!"* he shouted back. *"Confidence, Tiff!"*

The egos in the boat were immense. Shealy and Cashin would argue from time to time about which one was better, an argument that ended with an admission of mutual need. Wood showed his ego with the near-violence with which he rowed. Nothing showed the ego conflicts so much as the election of a captain at the end of their junior year. There were four clear candidates: Shealy, Cashin, Wood and Stone. None of them would vote for the others, and each probably voted for himself. No one in the jayvee boat would vote for any of the four. The compromise candidate became Blair Brooks, the relatively mild-mannered two-oar.

Behind all the hype and all the internal tension, Shealy thought, there had been something wonderful about being a part of those crews. A good crew meant shoehorning some eighteen hundred pounds of meat and ambition and ego into a thin shell that weighed about 180 pounds and then making it work. But in the case of a great crew, there was something glorious. Shealy believed that all people sought symmetry and purpose in their lives, something that lifted them up and made them feel better about themselves; and here were eight oarsmen, having worked so hard and sacrificed so much, catching something magical and doing it race after race, each oarsman making the others better. The feeling made them not just confident but also complete, and it was magnified by the knowledge that what they were accomplishing was pure in its amateurism. They were doing this because they wanted to, for no reward other than the feeling itself.

After rowing in those great Harvard boats and then in different international regattas in both fours and eights, Wood had moved over to sculling. There was a certain inevitability to that move. Not only was the national-champion sculler acknowleded as the best American rower, but at a more pragmatic level it was simply easier, as one got older and took on greater responsibilities, to be a sculler, just as it was easier to play tennis than to play baseball. A sculler could work out at whatever hours he fancied, adjusting his athletic routine to his work schedule; a member of a team had to practice when his teammates could.

In 1976, after Wood's friend Gregg Stone had gone to the Montreal Olympics as a tourist, he had suggested to Wood, who had made the team as a spare for the sweep oarsmen, that they try a double together. Stone had already done a fair amount of sculling, once a week as a senior while on the varsity crew and more frequently while he was in law school; for Wood, sculling was a new experience. In the fall of 1976, with only three days of practice together, they had entered the Head of the Charles, which was a major regatta. They had surprised themselves by taking second, beating, among others, Jim Dietz and Larry Klecatsky, who had often been the champions in the past. The following year, in 1977, they went to Henley and took second behind the British double that had been second in the 1976 Olympics.

In 1977 they had been ready to row in the national double trials, but Wood had become sick and they had been forced to cancel. Both had decided to enter the single trials two weeks later. Stone thought he was rowing very well. In his trial heat he had been pitted against Jim Dietz, who had placed fifth in the Olympic singles in 1972 at Munich and seventh at Montreal in 1976 and was just coming to the end of a career in which he had towered over all other American scullers. Dietz had gone out quickly and had won. But after the race Stone had told Wood that he was sure he could have won but had decided to hold back a little for the finals. Wood had also raced in that trial, but he had not made the final. Stone, rowing better and better, had beaten Dietz and become the champion the next day. If his victory had surprised almost everyone in the world of sculling, it had not surprised Stone. But the triumph had affected his and Wood's plans for a double; they might row together occasionally, but Stone was now the single-scull champion, and that remained his priority even after he and Wood won the U.S. national championship in 1978. A year later Stone, who had not done well in his international racing, was ready to concentrate on the double again, but the boat never moved as well.

Wood, rowing the double with Chris Allsopp, had taken fifth in the world championship in 1978. Wood was confident that he was becoming a better and more accomplished sculler, that he was making the slow transition from sweep oarsman to sculler right on schedule. In 1979 he had rowed in a good quad with Shealy, Allsopp and John Van Blon. That boat had *moved*. The total was clearly greater than the sum of the parts. They were relatively young scullers, the Olympics were looming ahead and they all had high hopes for what they could do in the quad in 1980. In the fall of 1979, Wood won the Head of the Charles in the single, which stamped him as a premier sculler. At the same time Stone, his friend, teammate and boatmate, was beginning to pull back from competition. Shealy, who was sharing a house with Stone, thought that the difference was that Stone had reached his limits and wanted to go on to other things.

But Wood's limits were as yet undefined. So he pushed himself relentlessly in those years, training with unusual austerity.

When the Olympic boycott shattered their hopes for the quad, Shealy and some of his other friends withdrew from the team to make the adjustment to more traditional lives. (Along the way Shealy had spent two years at Oxford and had made an ill-fated attempt to try out as a wide receiver for the Cleveland Browns.) But Wood was pushing into new frontiers for himself. Everything was coming together for him as a sculler; he had waited his turn behind Dietz and Stone, and in 1980 it seemed that his time had finally come. Then, in the spring of 1981, John Biglow had showed up on the Charles.

CHAPTER
EIGHT

Tiff Wood had heard of Biglow, of course. Wood was Harvard class of 1975, and Biglow was Yale class of 1980, but rowers knew of each other, and Wood knew that Biglow had been an extraordinary Yale oarsman who had stroked a great and favored Yale crew in a race against Harvard in 1979 that Harvard had won by 4 seconds. Many who had witnessed it, including Harry Parker, considered it probably the greatest race in the two schools' history. Four seconds over four miles was very little, and everyone had been aware of Biglow's remarkable resilience that day. Time and again when Harvard had made its move and had threatened to row through Yale, Biglow had refused to concede and had brought Yale back.

Tiff Wood knew that Biglow was supposed to be good, but he did not take Biglow seriously, since it was his first year in a single scull and he would clearly have to serve his apprenticeship before becoming serious competition. Besides, Wood had already had one previous experience with Biglow. In 1979 they had both been on the national team; and Biglow, who was supposed to have stroked the eight, had become sick and had not been able to row. Biglow had not dealt well with his inability to compete. Tiff Wood's impression of him had been of a gray-faced, sad young man always about to burst into tears. If there was one thing of which Tiff Wood had been sure after that regatta, it was that he would never see John Biglow on a national team again.

In the spring of 1981, Wood had been beating everyone on the Charles, including Stone, and had been rowing almost dead even with a very good woman's four. He was twenty-eight and stronger than he had ever been. He could literally feel his power increasing. Near the end of a race there was simply more strength to summon. He was also more disciplined than ever and more sure of his love for rowing. When Biglow showed up, only twenty-three at the time, Wood had found him a pleasant, modest young man, and they had begun to row together in practice. One day they had done a series of 2-minute pieces. A piece is a given section of a workout, and pieces are usually done in practice as a series of repetitions. Because Biglow was not supposed to be as good as Wood, Biglow had begun with a little head start. On the first four pieces Wood had passed him, but on the fifth and sixth pieces Wood suddenly realized that he was no longer gaining on Biglow. On the last piece Biglow had realized what was happening and without either of them saying anything, they had started out even.

That night, Wood had rowed back and sat in the boathouse and thought, "Oh, he's really good. He is very, very good." Later Biglow had come into the boathouse, and Wood had told him he had rowed very well. "You were beating me on some of those pieces today," he had said very quietly. Clearly the challenger had arrived.

Two days later they had rowed again, doing fifteen-hundred-meter pieces, and Biglow had beaten Wood on all three. Even more ominously for Wood, there had been a double out that day with Shealy and Stone in it. Although it was not a championship double, it was nonetheless a double, with two very accomplished oarsmen in it. In one of the pieces the double had rowed against the two singles. Shealy and Stone had given the two singles head starts, and then gradually the double had started catching up. With five hundred meters to go, Biglow had turned it on, racing all out, and he had managed to stay ahead of the double. Wood, watching, knew he was in serious trouble, but he consoled himself with the fact that though Biglow clearly was a very talented oar, he was nonetheless new at it and had not raced in competition before. That was a very different matter. There were lots of men who looked good in practice and were not quite as good in races. Wood prided himself that his strength was in the races themselves. Wood decided that Biglow would have to wait his turn.

A few weeks later they had rowed against each other in the New England regional championship in Hanover. In the heat, which neither needed to win, Biglow had been slightly ahead at the end, with both of them coasting. Biglow had turned and said, "Gee, this isn't too hard." The remark had annoyed Wood, who had been content until then to let Biglow win the heat, and Wood had sprinted for the finish. In the final there was room for only three lanes, and Joe Bouscaren had rowed in the third lane. If it was the first time the three of them had ever rowed in singles against each other, it was by no means the last. Wood had gone out very quickly and very hard, at a thirty-eight, an unusually high stroke. He had kept it there for the first five hundred yards, and for all of that he was only three quarters of a length ahead of Biglow. Then in the second five hundred Biglow had almost rowed through Wood. But Wood had held on, determined not to be psychologically defeated, as would be so easy, having put out so much and gotten back so small a lead. With five hundred meters left, when they were almost dead even, Wood started to sprint. That meant Biglow had to respond, and they had rowed almost side by side for five hundred meters, matching stroke for stroke, neither conceding, neither taking the stroke up, each simply trying to put more power into each stroke. It was an almost perfect race, and both Wood and Biglow had been hypnotically fascinated by it. This was the hardest kind of race because there was no way to back down. The pain in Biglow's arms and legs had been so terrible that he had wished that Wood would either surge ahead or fade and spare him all of this.

Normally, in any race, there is a moment when the pain becomes too great and one of the racers either physically or psychologically, it does not matter, cracks. It does not have to be a very big crack, just one rower making his surge, pouring everything in and breaking either his competitor or himself. But neither racer faltered. They simply matched strokes for the last third of the race. Biglow decided that the only way to continue was to think of one stroke at a time, that and nothing more. Only then could he keep rowing. They crossed the finish line in a dead heat, although the angle of the finish line favored Biglow. Bouscaren was far behind. "Good race, John," Wood said to his opponent. Good race, he thought, hell, it was almost perfect.

For Wood the experience had been exhilarating. Quite possibly he had rowed an almost perfect race. He had rowed his absolute best and found someone he could not row through. Anyone else would have come apart in that race. He is a wonderful oar, Wood had thought, just a wonderful oar. Later that day Wood realized he had mixed feelings. Part of him was a little sad because he had lost, and part of him felt profoundly enhanced because he had been a principal in something so nearly perfect. Biglow, he realized, was not going to have to wait for a year or two. He had already arrived.

Nonetheless, Wood was still confident he could beat Biglow but was careful not to practice with him anymore. He believed that since he was experienced and Biglow was not, joint practices helped Biglow gain confidence. Tiff Wood saw no need to improve John Biglow's confidence. That race in Hanover had been quite enough of a contribution.

Biglow was, of course, very pleased that he had won, and somewhat surprised that he had come on so quickly as a sculler. Single sculling was not supposed to be like this. He was not supposed to beat the top sculler in the country in his first race. In rowing it was proper to ascend slowly, not win from the start. In the trials later that year, he and Wood had been in the same heat. The winner would go to the finals, everyone else to the repechage. In the heat Wood had been about a half length behind Biglow with five hundred meters to go when Biglow hit a buoy. Wood had heard the crack of the oar and then the sound of Biglow catching a crab, and he had immediately turned on all his power and had taken a quick length lead to win the heat. That had sent Wood directly to the finals and Biglow to the repechage. The heat had been in the morning, the rep was in the afternoon and the final was the next morning. In the final Wood still felt sore in his legs from his race the previous day, and he had gone out at a low rate. He had heard Harry Parker in the background shouting to take the stroke up. Bouscaren had held the early lead, and then Biglow had just rowed right through him and through Wood. That had taught Tiff Wood that Biglow was special, that his endurance was exceptional and that he became stronger as a regatta went on.

In the months after that they became not just competitors but also good friends. They loved rowing against each other in practice. The pleasure was special. No one could push Wood like Biglow, and no one could push Biglow like Wood. Off the water they were unlikely friends; but bonded as they were by this sport, by the fact that what each liked best in those spring days was to row against the other, they became closer and closer. The time was the most productive either had ever known on the water, and while Biglow was winning most of the longer pieces, they were astonishingly even. Each could feel himself improving every day. Wood knew they were both going very fast, and he was confident when Biglow left for Europe that summer that he was going to do very well in international competition. Wood's admiration for Biglow grew, as a competitor and as a man. John, he thought, was an oarsman of complete integrity. He gave everything he had on every stroke and he never cheated. Biglow in turn felt protected by Wood, who was older, more mature and more confident and who now openly shared everything he had. It was like having a wonderful older rowing brother.

CHAPTER
NINE

This spring their workouts were taking place under the eye of Harry Parker. To Wood, who had rowed for him in different capacities for thirteen years, he was a singular figure of authority. The most natural thing in the world was to go up to Newell Boathouse and work out for three or four hours and then wait to hear a few pithy but prized words from Harry. For Biglow and Bouscaren he was a figure even more shrouded in the mystique of winning, for in their college years Yale had probably had better crews and Harvard had nonetheless always won. Biglow approached Parker as if he knew some sort of final secret that once passed on would guarantee success.

But even without this mystique, Parker was a dominating personality. As these oarsmen readied themselves for the Olympic trials, he, more than anyone else, was in their thoughts and they talked constantly about him—what his mood was, whom he was paying attention to, what signals (however small) he might be sending out.

In another sport what a coach felt might not mean so much; but in rowing, where everything was so subtle, where it was so difficult to calibrate the differences among oarsmen, all of whom looked powerful, the coach's views were even more crucial. When coaches in other sports had great teams, star athletes shared much of the credit. One thought of the great John Wooden basketball teams and one thought not just of Wooden but of Jabbar and Walton as well, of Bear Bryant and his superb quarterbacks Joe Namath and Ken Stabler. But in rowing, a great crew's glory was divided by eight, and so the towering figure was the coach, particularly a coach who won year after year. There was an implicit belief that if a young man turned into a great oarsman, somehow Harry Parker had helped shape him.

In other sports several sources of power and authority existed for the great athlete. There was the college coach and then the professional coach. There was the agent. There were the media, which could cast glory upon the athlete rather than upon the coach, making the athlete inevitably freer and more independent of the coach. None of that was true of rowing. If in America and American sports, sources of authority in all walks of life had been divided as new sources of power arose, that was not true of rowing. The sources of power were frozen as they might have been fifty years ago. Harry Parker was not just the coach of the Harvard crew but he was often the coach of the national team, making him, in effect, both the college and the professional coach as well. Now he was the coach of the Olympic sculling team.

He was as much myth as man. His decisions, however arbitrary they might seem to disappointed oarsmen, had a finality that left those who questioned them outsiders. For almost twenty years no one ruled the sport as Harry Parker did. When Harvard was late to a race against Northeastern one year, the Northeastern coach, somewhat edgy, had asked where Parker was. The answer had been that Harry was walking over, but he would be a little late because he had tripped on a few boathouses on the way.

His nature did not encourage intimacy. Intimacy diminished his power as the distance he kept enhanced it. There were, as one of his oarsmen said, veils of privacy around him, and one did not lightly try to remove them. There was no Mr. Chips to him. He did not become buddies with his oarsmen even after they graduated, yet his pride in them was immense. He knew he was a central figure in their lives—indeed, often *the* central figure—but this did not mean they were close. For a long time he did not even go to the weddings of his former oarsmen, though by the mid-1970s he relaxed this policy. When one young bride, aware of how much this meant to her husband, that *Harry* had come to their wedding, had effusively thanked him, he had seemed surprised. "But this is where I should be this weekend," he had said.

He did not give emotional prerace speeches, and he did not exhort his crews for the greater glory of Harvard or the infamy of Yale. Members of one of his great Olympic crews could remember him coming up before the final and saying simply, "Well, there are a lot of good crews out there today, so if you want to win, you'll really have to dig in and get it." His crews did not go out on the water in a rah-rah manner to win one for good old Harry. Rather, they feared to measure up to his standards. His great triumph was that he forced his oarsmen to find what they were looking for within themselves. It was not that he was without emotion about the immense sacrifice and hardship that these young men endured; he simply could not easily express it. At the annual dinner of the Friends of Harvard Rowing, a fund raiser for the sport of Harvard at which he was always the principal speaker, he often broke into tears talking of what had happened in the previous year.

There was a genuine wariness about him, as if he were always on the alert for fraud or con. His eyes constantly measured the people around him, wondering what they really wanted and what price they would pay, whether they were as tough as he was. His face was weatherbeaten and rugged. This reporter looking at him, measuring him as he measured others, thought of him more likely as a great battalion commander. He was a ferocious competitor and he almost single-handedly had changed the nature of American rowing. Before his arrival, it had been a sport practiced from March through June each year. After his arrival, the Harvard crews practiced year-round; and when they soon ruled the sport, other crews practiced year-round as well. The force of his personality left nothing to challenge. What Harry said, went. He might have countless enemies outside Harvard, particularly around Philadelphia, a great center of rowing, and there might be anti-Parker feeling among men whose crews he had beaten or who had failed to make a national team he was coaching. But at Harvard, he was a law unto himself.

His crews pushed themselves because they were good and knew they were good, but also because Harry Parker pushed them. They were an extension of him and his ferocious desire to win. It was not so much what Harry said as what he didn't say. Harry did not just coach them, he competed with them. If their sport was in large measure in trying to find out what the human limits were, then Harry somehow was the self-appointed arbiter of those limits. He made the stadium runs with them, elbowing them if he thought he had a chance to edge ahead. If the Hobbs brothers, Bill and Fritz, were taking out a pair and if Harry was rowing against them in a single scull, there was no doubt that it was not just a workout but also a race that Harry did not intend to lose—and never did. When the Harvard crew went to New London to prepare for the four-mile race against Yale, they played, for lack of something better to do, croquet; and in these croquet games Parker was, in Shealy's words, "devious as hell—a notorious cheat, always changing the rules to suit his own situation." In the late 1970s one of his assistant coaches, a young man named Peter Raymond, had once gone to the stadium for a workout and Parker had suggested that they run together. Raymond, some fifteen years younger, realized in the middle of the workout that Parker was not just running with him but that he was also running against him, that he *had* to win. The intensity of Parker's drive had unnerved Raymond; it seemed so much invested in so little. On certain fall afternoons the Harvard and Boston University crews would practice together, and afterward they would have soccer games in which Harry Parker was the most violent player on the field, throwing elbows with abandon. One afternoon there was an air ball, and Harry and a B.U. player went for it at the same time and collided. Harry chipped a tooth in half but kept right on playing. He loved rowing against this crew in singles and could, in his midforties, beat most of them. Once he entered the Head of the Charles regatta under the name of T. Lazarus, the man who had come back from the dead. He was just as fanatic as a cross-country skier; in 1978, he entered a forty-kilometer cross-country ski meet in weather that never rose above ten below. At every check-point there were doctors looking for frostbite. Parker managed with great skill to keep his totally white ear from the view of the doctors. His competitiveness fed his team's competitiveness, and theirs fed his. Madness begot madness.

Most of these young men, coming as they did from affluent homes of comfort and kindness, had never before encountered a set of rules and standards so demanding and a man who so embodied those standards. Praise was rare from him, and because it was rare, it was all the more valued. Thus the less he said, the more his credibility increased. His strength was in his distance, the fact that they had to reach for him as he could not reach for them, and by reaching for him they met his standards. He dealt with them without con and manipulation. Tiff Wood believed he had too much respect for his oarsmen to play any games, to try to gain even a small advantage by either abusing or praising an oarsman. His praise was always careful. When the Rude and Smooth won victory after victory, its members began to debate among themselves whether they were the greatest crew in Harvard history, or at least the greatest crew Harry had coached. Even more, they wondered whether Harry would finally come out and say *it*, that this was the greatest crew he had ever coached. The previous standard, they knew, had been the 1967–68 crew, which had gone to the Olympics and had been favored to win a gold before several of its members became sick. By their junior year the Rude and Smooth members eagerly picked up every newspaper after each win to see whether Harry had finally said it. He never said it. He said other things, which by his standards were almost lavish, such as "that was a very well-rowed race today." But he never said the one thing they wanted.

Those who had rowed for him in college thought he was a perfectly situated man, coaching rowing at a school such as Harvard, dealing with proud, highly intelligent, self-motivated athletes. In a commercial world, he was able to create an environment where exceptional young men sacrificed themselves neither for love nor for money but for certain goals and a certain pride. The true victory for one of his oarsmen was not over the person next to you or the person in another boat but over his standards. Above all, he sensed why it was that they were amateurs, why they gave so much in a society that gave back so little reward. For his men, rowing was as much theology as sport; it was built entirely upon faith. The oarsman's self-esteem and membership in this elite circle depended completely on what he did; if he worked hard enough, he would be rewarded.

Parker seemed, if anything, somewhat out of tune with the latter part of this century. He was clearly highly intelligent, completely driven and very subtle. He was not a man to cross. His presence was austere and demanding. It was impossible to think of a profession—corporate management, academia, medicine—where he would not have risen to the very top. Yet he had remained a coach, poorly paid by contemporary standards, in a spot far from the center of contemporary athletic excitement. But he loved what he did and never found himself bored. There was nothing he might covet that he did not have, no other person he would rather be. The only time he had felt his lack of affluence had come a few years earlier, when he had got divorced and it had become clear to him how little money he made compared to what comparably successful and driven men made. But that reaction quickly passed.

The greatest role model in his life, Joe Burk, the coach at Penn, had done the same thing, and he was, he knew, in many ways the lineal descendant of Joe Burk. Burk was a man of a less complicated time, when there were more rules and fewer opportunities to break them. He was born in 1914 and had been a great oarsman as both a sweep oar and a sculler. He had graduated from Penn and gone to work on the family fruit farm in New Jersey. He worked the farm during the week, and on weekends he drove to nearby regattas, took his scull off his car, went out and rowed and won, put his scull back on his car and drove back to his farm. He did not sit around and talk with the other rowing buffs and have a drink with them. He had no need for that. He was a loner, completely independent, largely self-taught as an oarsman (though later it turned out he had corresponded with George Pocock, the great oarsman and builder of sculls in Seattle).

Burk believed that every oarsman had to find out what felt right for himself. He favored the sheer use of power, while traditionalists such as Pocock spoke of rowing as a symphony of motion. Burk believed there was too much emphasis on technique, as if finesse alone had some mystical capacity to move boats. What moved boats were power and endurance. He was in perfect condition; the farm was just far enough south to allow him to row year-round. In the summer he liked to row up Rancocas Creek to the Delaware River, where he usually encountered big weekend powerboats. He would sprint against them, delighting in the bewildered voices of those aboard who could not understand how this little boat with one man rowing could keep ahead of them. Most scullers in those days raced at about twenty-eight strokes to the minute, a pace that permitted perfect form but was low in terms of energy. In about 1936, Joe Burk went to a much higher number of strokes, thirty-six, and every year after that, he took it up a stroke or two until he was racing at forty-two, turning races into sprints. In the late 1930s he was the best sculler in America, quite possibly in the world; he had come in second during the 1936 American trials when he was only twenty-two, and for a period of about four years he did not lose a single race. Everyone assumed he would be the Olympic champion in 1940 and 1944, but there were no Olympics in those years. Parker considered him the perfect amateur. When an Australian sculler named Bobby Pearce, who had won the Olympics in both 1928 and 1932, challenged him to some races, Burk declined. He wanted to meet Pearce, but he had a powerful sense that the events would not be as clean as they should, that too much was going to be bet, as had happened in sculling challenges in the 1870s. Rowing should be done only for its own sake.

In 1951, he was hired to coach at Penn. He was an oddly formal man; he wore three-piece suits and kept his distance from most of his athletes. Coaching a winning crew was a serious business, his manner implied. There were curfew hours, and his crews would keep them. When Harry Parker as a sophomore told a boatmate that it would be all right to stay up an additional hour, Burk was furious with Parker. How dare Parker do this? How dare he put himself above Burk's rules? A year later, one of the varsity oarsmen was immediately demoted to the jayvee boat for drinking a few beers. When the Penn crews went to West Germany, they were not allowed to drink Coke at receptions because it was carbonated, nor could they imbibe spirits even after their last triumphant victory. Joe Burk did not want people's final memory of his athletes to be one of noisy young Americans careening drunkenly through hotel chambers. There were dress codes, ties and jackets to be worn and, later, in the 1960s, hair codes (he used a dowel to check hair length). He set weight limits for his athletes and weighed them once a week. If they were over their appointed weight, they ran three or four miles. If, at the end of the winter, there was a question whether the water was too cold to row on (in case something happened and a boat sank), Joe Burk settled the question by diving in the water.

In 1953, Harry Parker, then eighteen years old, walked into Joe Burk's world. Parker came from East Hartford, Connecticut, on a naval scholarship. He wanted badly to be an athlete but had always lacked the requisite natural skills. He had played basketball in high school, but to no great advantage. When he registered on his first day at Penn, the crew coaches standing in line behind the Penn administrators were eyeing any young man who was six feet tall and suggesting that he might want to row. Harry Parker paid no attention until he reached the end of the line, where another Penn administrator asked him whether he was going to take phys-ed courses or a sport. "I'm going to be a rower," he immediately announced. "The tanks are down that way," said the man, pointing to the bowels of the athletic building. So he became a rower.

Parker liked the sense of power he felt as his oar moved through water. Like Tiff Wood years later, he sensed immediately that this was something he could be good at, that its basic requirement was passion and dedication. In his freshman year he weighed 160 pounds and rowed on the lightweight crew. By chance Joe Burk was coaching the freshman lights that year, and by his sophomore year Parker was in the varsity heavy boat. Joe Burk had found his protégé.

Burk had a sense that Parker's physical commitment was exceptional. But there was something more than just physical commitment. One of Burk's earliest memories of Harry Parker was of a young man working on his oar in the tank. Parker was gritting his teeth so hard that he drew blood, and even though the blood was running down his mouth, he paid no attention to it. He just kept on rowing. No one Burk had ever coached had as much passion for rowing, not just to do it but also to live it all the time. On weekends Parker and a friend would walk the eight miles to Burk's suburban house to talk rowing. Parker kept complete logs of everything he had done as an oarsman, and these logs reflected a remarkable knowledge of the sport. They were a coach's logs.

Without realizing it, Parker had modeled his life on

Burk's. Like Burk, Parker was reserved and aloof yet passionate. He had felt at home with Burk because this was so natural a manner for him. He was emulating what he already was. He had entered Penn thinking he would become an engineer, but he had fallen in love with his liberal-arts courses and decided he would go into teaching when he graduated. But he owed time to the Navy for his ROTC scholarship, and guided by Burk, he moved over to sculling while in the Navy. Joe Burk taught Harry Parker how to scull, and it was said that in the late 1950s, when the two of them went out every day, Burk, by then in his midforties, could still take a length lead on the younger Parker and hold it every time. ("I think that was true," said Parker, "though we weren't *really* racing. The amazing thing is that ten years later he was still doing that to the top scullers in the area.") Parker did better against others, becoming the Pan-Am champion in 1959 and the American sculler at the 1960 Olympics, where he was automatically in the shadow of Vyacheslav Ivanov, the great Soviet oarsman.

With the possible exception of Pertti Karppinen of Finland, Ivanov was the greatest sculler Harry Parker had ever seen. If someone had been designing the prototype of the sculler, he would have designed Ivanov. He was six-four, long-limbed, immensely powerful in the back and legs, with great endurance. He was also beautifully coached. When Parker went to Rome in 1960, Ivanov already had the first of his three gold medals, which he had won at Melbourne in 1956 at the age of eighteen in an extraordinary race with his only true rival of that era, Stuart McKenzie of Australia.

Their exceptional rivalry, which lasted for several years, eventually flowered into real friendship. If Ivanov was perfectly built for rowing, McKenzie was not. He had a barrel chest, long arms that seemed to swing down to his knees, and curiously clumsy body movements. In the Melbourne race, McKenzie, then only nineteen himself, had taken a huge early lead and had stayed in front almost the entire race. Near the end, Ivanov had made what was to become his patented move, an all-out charge. Steadily he passed boat after boat. When he passed Jack Kelly, who was second, he had a sense that Kelly turned his face away so that Ivanov would not see the pain in it. Steadily Ivanov gained on McKenzie. Then, right near the end, McKenzie stopped rowing for a moment. He simply had nothing left. A split second later Ivanov, equally exhausted, stopped. Then both resumed. But Ivanov was just a little bit ahead and won.

A year later, McKenzie took his revenge. The two were at Henley, and they were playing chess together. In the middle of the chess game, McKenzie gave Ivanov quite an odd look. He had just learned something crucial about his opponent. Ivanov, he had decided, played chess the same way he rowed. He cannot play methodically— he needs the cavalry charge. With that, McKenzie decided to go to a much higher plateau of speed against Ivanov, to exhaust him so there would be no final burst. It worked. He won the Henley race by .02 second. Ivanov jumped out of his boat and swam over to congratulate McKenzie; but rattled by the defeat, Ivanov rowed poorly for the next two years, constantly changing his pace.

By 1960, he had regained his rhythm. He and McKenzie, good friends now, worked out before the 1960 Olympics on Lake Albano, and McKenzie realized he could not possibly beat Ivanov. McKenzie had one silver, and he did not seek another. He did not row in the Olympics, but Harry Parker did.

Ivanov, then twenty-two and in the Soviet Army, was a figure of awe to Parker. The Olympics being about friendship and fellowship, they even had a brief conversation. Some of the Soviet sweep oarsmen were Lithuanians who still thought of themselves as Lithuanians and who spoke a little English. They told Parker that Ivanov badly wanted to meet his American competitor, and they coached him in what to say. Parker, good Olympian, had memorized these words and gone over to Ivanov. They had shaken hands. Ivanov had beamed with fraternal sports pleasure. Parker had beamed with fraternal sports pleasure. "*Sukin syn*," Parker had said in his instant Russian. Ivanov's face had fallen, and he had become chilly. A decade later, watching the scene in the movie *Patton* where the general said the same thing to the Russian generals, he realized he had said "you son-of-a-bitch" to Ivanov. It had not been so fraternal after all. In the intervening years, Harry Parker had thought often of Ivanov; the one thing Parker was almost certain of was that Ivanov had not been sent to Afghanistan with other Soviet troops.

Coming out of the Navy, still subtly guided by Burk, Parker decided to take a job as the freshman rowing coach at Harvard. It was a pleasant place, where he could work on a Ph.D. and coach at the same time. He believed the job would be temporary. Temporary it was. Two years later, the Harvard varsity rowing coach, Harvey Love, died of a heart attack, and Harry Parker was named head coach. He was twenty-eight. That year, 1963, Yale was heavily favored. Harvard won. It won the next eighteen times in a row. Thus began the myth.

CHAPTER
TEN

So on the weekend in Princeton he was coach of all the scullers. His Harvard crews would have to wait. Most of the top scullers had been working out in Cambridge, where the facilities were particularly good. Parker had tried to be meticulous in not favoring his former Harvard oarsmen, something he was often accused of by disappointed non-Harvard rowers. He knew the strengths and weaknesses of each of the competitors. Biglow had powers of concentration that were complete. He was totally unflappable before a race, he never doubted his ability and he loved to race. As long as he believed in himself, he would be all right. He was not as smooth a rower as he should have been, but his strength and his sense of purpose made up for that.

What made Tiff Wood so strong was determination. There was no way that Tiff Wood could give any more than he did; he punished himself to the ultimate level. Two or three inches shorter than Biglow, Wood should not even have been a world-class sculler.

Bouscaren pushed himself just as hard as Wood but in other ways. Bouscaren was the smoothest of the three, and in the past year he had brought his endurance level up dramatically. He was bright and sensitive, quicker than the others to feel slighted, probably because he was not as big. In 1983, after Wood had won the singles, they had all gone to the national team's sculling camp. It had been an aggressive camp, and at one point Parker had tried both Biglow and Bouscaren in a double. Because their boat had not been particularly fast, Parker had moved Bouscaren out and another oarsmen in. Bouscaren had immediately gone to Parker and asked, "Do you think John is more effective in the team boats than I am?" So that's it, thought Parker. Bouscaren needed to have parity with Biglow; and as long as they were in the same boat, they were peers. If he was out of the boat, there was a problem.

Roughly forty young men were competing in the single-scull trial; another forty were rowing doubles in races that would entitle them, if they did well, to go to the sculling camp and compete for the double or the quad. Theirs were not official races; however, the single trial was. The first day of racing, Friday, was devoted to the heats. There were seven heats, with six or seven oarsmen in each. The winner of each heat would automatically advance to the semifinals. The others, in case the heats had been unfairly seeded, would row in the repechage the next morning. There would be six heats in the reps, and the winner of each would also be in the semifinals. The problem, of course, was that the semis would be rowed later that day.

Few surprises were likely in Friday's heats. Wood and Biglow were considered cofavorites for the final, with Bouscaren just a shade behind. The second tier consisted of Jim Dietz, the former U.S. single sculling champion, and Brad Lewis, who had rowed in the U.S. national double the previous year and who had worked out the past winter in California.

Jim Dietz was thirty-five, and he had been rowing competitively since he was seventeen. He had twice been the American single sculler at the Olympics, in 1972 and 1976. He had not been a major figure in sculling since 1980, but in 1983, with the Olympics beginning to appear on the horizon, he had started to push himself again, and in the 1983 American single trials he had come in second to Tiff Wood,

4.4 seconds behind, beating both Bouscaren and Biglow.
Until the 1983 race he had been trying to wean himself from
rowing by taking a job on the American Stock Exchange.
But his 1983 race had been too encouraging. The flame of
Olympic glory had flickered just enough to keep him rowing.
In 1984 he had been rowing a lot of miles, but he had not
really been racing—that is, punishing himself. He thought
he knew the field better than anyone else; they had been be-
ginners coming forward when he had been in his prime. He
considered Wood the strongest; if they raced five times, he
was sure Wood would win at least three races. But he also
thought Wood vulnerable. There was immense pressure on
him as the defending champion; and everyone was gunning
for him, a position Dietz knew all too well from his own
years as a champion. In a single, winner-take-all race, what
he hoped to do was catch the younger men by surprise while
they were preoccupied with each other, row one great race
and win. He believed he had that one great race in him; his
problem was that it took him longer and longer to recuperate. If he was caught in a tough heat, he would use up his
energy there. That was his problem. More than anything
else, he had to conserve his energy.

ELEVEN

The other rower in what was generally considered the second tier was Brad Lewis. The word from California by way of the rowing grapevine (Mike Livingston, a former Harvard oarsman, had been coaching him, and Mike's brother Cleve was living in Cambridge and still rowing and connected to everyone at the Harvard boathouse) was that Brad Lewis was rowing very well. But in the past he had shown a tendency to wear out; and besides, he was from California and practiced there rather than in the East. In a sport where regional prejudices were powerful, he was not taken quite as seriously as if he had been rowing on the Charles. It was all right to *be* from California, no one could really help that, but to continue to train there indicated that an oarsman was probably not entirely serious. It hinted at an inverted value system; for in a world where the Puritan ethic was as operative as it was in rowing, the idea of California, particularly *Southern* California, conjured up visions, no matter how unconscious, of a softer and more indulgent life-style.

Lewis was a complicated and sometimes difficult young man. He was not at ease with the other oarsmen, who were eastern in shape, form and manner, and they in turn found him moody. He was passionate about the world of rowing and largely estranged from most of the others who inhabited it. This year he was almost pleased that no one was taking him that seriously.

He wanted to surprise them during the single trials. He had virtually sneaked into Princeton and had made no effort to be sociable. On the first day when he had gone out on the water, Joe Bouscaren had rowed by. "Hey, Brad," he had said, genuinely pleased to see him, "how are you?" Lewis had not answered. "Come on, Brad," Bouscaren had said, "say hello." Still there was silence. Lewis kept rowing. "Stop rowing!" Bouscaren said. "Now! Stop rowing!" "I can't," Lewis said, "I'm in the middle of a piece." He rowed by. Well, thought Bouscaren, that's Brad, still psyching himself up. Brad Lewis, who hoped to be the *other* Lewis at the Olympic games, the one who did not get on the cover of *Time* magazine, was appalled by the idea that the other competing scullers had traveled to Princeton with their rivals, Biglow with Bouscaren, Wood with Altekruse.

Lewis's concept of rowing did not permit such fraternization with the enemy, and to him, the men he was rowing against for something as precious as this were the enemy. If most of the other oarsmen, such as Wood and Biglow, pushed themselves into rowing because they wanted to belong to something, wanted the camaraderie and a form of social acceptance, Brad Lewis pushed himself because he wanted to remain apart. The Lewis men, said his cousin Mitch Lewis, who accompanied him as his coach, therapist and trainer, are independent. They do not like being a part of things and get nervous in organizational charts. They will work very hard for something as long as no one tells them what to do. "I think we're black sheep," he said. "We always have trouble with coaches. We love to do what people tell us we can't do, and we don't like to do what people tell us we should do."

Brad Lewis's home life had not been an easy one. His mother had been very sick when he was young, and he was raised largely by his father. Out of that, his friends thought, came a certain edginess and defensiveness. Brad was highly sensitive to slights and oddly insensitive to what he did to others. His behavior with others was unusually provocative. By being rude to his colleagues, by alienating them and turning them against him, he was creating the self-fulfilling prophecy he wanted—that he was largely alone against the world. He acted as though someone were going to take advantage of him unless he took advantage first. He had a strong sense of grievance and disliked being beholden to anyone. "I hate," he once told a friend, "having to ask for things, having to say please to people and having to say thank you." It was not easy to be his friend or, for that matter, even his teammate.

A year earlier, when he had made the national team in the double, his partner, Paul Enquist, had found sustaining the friendship required for a double to be one of the hardest things he had ever done. There had been long periods when Lewis barely spoke to Enquist, and sometimes Brad treated him as if he were an opponent, not a teammate.

On this weekend Lewis saw himself as a warrior, stalking the enemy. The enemy were Tiff Wood (whom, almost alone among the scullers, he actually liked) and then Bouscaren and possibly Biglow as well. Lewis knew that the Easterners did not think of him as a peer, but that did not bother him. He was convinced that his picture and a feature article about him would never grace the pages of *The Oarsman* (or as it was now called, *Rowing USA*), the publication of the U.S. Rowing Association. That feeling was shared by many West Coast oarsmen, a belief that in a sport where there was little outside public attention they failed to get even peer recognition.

In Lewis's formative years in sculling, the other oarsmen had been Easterners; they had gone to school with each other, they had their own network and they put each other up during regattas. He had been the outsider. He was young, he did not have a lot of money and his manners were almost deliberately rough. They had complained that, if he came and stayed with you, he stayed too long and did not readily contribute for the food. They had called him "America's Guest." It was not that others were probably any less self-obsessed; it was only that they were better at disguising it. Lewis was aware that social situations were not easy for him; and as far as he was concerned, the smaller the group the better. With six other people he became eerily silent, retreating into himself and making the rest uneasy. To his peers, he seemed not just different but even defiant and on occasion boastful. In 1983, when he had come back to Boston to prepare for the single-scull trials, he kept telling people he was going to win. It was possible that this might happen, but in the code of rowing, one did not go around saying it would. It was considered bad form, particularly since, as it happened, he did not win. A year later, at the sculling camp, John Biglow was talking with Lewis and mentioned the boast of the previous year and how it had grated on the other oarsmen. For a while Lewis did not say anything, but 10 minutes later he came over to Biglow, quite surprised, and asked, "Did that really bother you?"

It had been Lewis's own way of psyching himself to take on the dreaded Easterners. Despite the eastern snobbery toward California oarsmen, he thought that Californians had a genuine advantage over the Easterners. Californians could row all year, while the Easterners lost four or five months to the weather. The erg, the weight room and the tank might be acceptable substitutes for rowing, but nothing was better for oarsmen, he believed, than real rowing on real water. He was sure that in the past year he had rowed twice as many miles as anyone else in the country. But even then he felt very much alone. As he worked out in Newport, supported only by himself and his father, he became increasingly suspicious of traditional coaching. As he improved and coaches who had once, in his mind, scorned him now began to show some interest, he approached them warily. In truth, he trusted only himself, his father and very few others in the world of rowing. He had, in fact, wanted, at one of the pre-Olympic races, to put a bumper sticker on his boat that said,

"Question Authority." He had been told that was not acceptable. The bumper sticker was gone, but the attitude remained.

On this weekend he was tracking Tiff Wood. He thought about Tiff all the time, what a strong racer and how mentally tough he was. Earlier in the year, Lewis had been finishing a workout in Newport Bay when a member of the harbor patrol who was his friend had signaled to him and he had rowed over. The patrolman had a copy of *Ultrasport*, a magazine devoted to athletes such as rowers and runners who pushed their bodies to the ultimate limit. "You see this?" the friend had asked. It was a huge takeout on Tiff Wood, and it told how well he was rowing. When Lewis finished reading the article, he turned around and rowed ten more miles that day.

The previous Christmas, Tiff had come out to Newport to row in the Christmas regatta, an 850-meter sprint. For Lewis it was an important test because Wood was the reigning champion, he had blazing speed and it was almost impossible to beat him in a sprint. Wood had beaten Lewis by a fraction, but Lewis had been encouraged. In his mind that close a finish meant he was on schedule, and he had the rest of the winter and spring to work out on real water.

He had several standards by which to measure his improvement. One was his clockings as he rowed every day around Lido Island in Newport Bay. These he called Lidos. His times for a Lido, which was 2½ miles, and for a Double Lido, which was five miles, had come down steadily in the past year. The water was remarkably calm, so the times were meaningful. The other measurement was how well he did in workouts against Hans Svensson, a Swedish sculler who had been fifth at the 1980 Olympics.

Svensson was a huge man and an accomplished sculler. In the fall of 1980, he had come to Southern California to escape the Swedish winter, and he and Lewis had worked out together. Svensson had absolutely dominated the American. In 1981, Svensson had returned. Though he still regularly beat Lewis, their races were a good deal closer, and Lewis could sometimes actually see the puddles from Svensson's oars. They were also becoming friends. Svensson had on occasion stayed with the Lewis family in Corona del Mar, a Newport Beach suburb, and Lewis had visited Svensson in Sweden (where he proved, by Svensson's account, a somewhat imperfect guest, complaining about the food and demanding, as a good Southern California boy should, an avocado; when Mrs. Svensson had found one, unlikely though that was in Sweden, he spit it out because it was served unripe).

The workouts had helped Lewis. Unlike most Americans, who eased into their workouts, Svensson worked hard from the moment his boat was on the water. He would take thirty strokes to limber up and then go all out. He did not coast or pace himself. In 1982, Lewis had beaten Svensson, for the first time, in the Christmas regatta. Generally, though, Svensson was still the winner over longer distances. Then in the fall of 1983—the perfect time for Lewis, who was preparing for the 1984 Olympic trials—he started beating Svensson regularly. The victories were sure signs to him that he had reached world-class status. The pieces had finally come together.

Tiff Wood thought that Brad Lewis was a fascinating man. For Brad, rowing was not just the critical experience, it was the *only* experience. Wood believed that because Lewis had no life other than rowing, any setback in rowing was doubly bitter for him, just as any victory was doubly exhilarating. Lewis largely agreed. He could not think of himself in any other terms than as a rower. It was not that he had a few lesser priorities; he had *no* other priorities. He judged a given day by how much it had helped his rowing.

He was twenty-nine in the summer of 1984, and any jobs he had held after college had lasted only long enough to let him earn the money that would permit him to continue rowing. He lived at home, and his father had helped support him. He had worked principally as a rough framer, building the outside of houses. In three or four months, he could make $6,000 or $7,000. That was the amount he needed for his sculling, for boats, for travel and meals. He owned four sculls, each worth $3,000 or $4,000. Some of the other scullers made fun of his penchant for equipment, but he liked keeping abreast of developments in boats and did not think four of them too heavy a commitment. For the past two years he had taken a job with the Wells Fargo bank under the Olympic Job Opportunity program, which allowed him to spend almost all his time rowing. He knew that the single-mindedness of his life, how little he gave to anything and anyone else, made him a selfish person, but until he achieved his goals, that was the way it was going to have to be.

Rowing was the only positive channel for the aggression and rebellion in him. He was willing to work very hard for something he wanted, but only on his own terms. Even in Little League baseball, there had been a constant series of conflicts with his coaches. In high school he might have played a variety of sports, but he had been wary of the ones where the coaches were always giving orders. He had tried basketball as a freshman but found the program filled with Mickey Mouse rules. He was not on the starting team, and the coach had a rule that none of the substitutes could sit down during practice. At one practice Lewis and another sub were sitting down. The coach looked over. "What are you two guys doing?" he asked. "Tell him," whispered the other boy, "that we're practicing for the next game." "We're getting ready for the next game," Lewis had said. That was his last basketball practice.

The rowing program, by contrast, had been relatively relaxed, and soon it had become a haven for some of the school's most talented but dissident athletes. Brad Lewis believed that he, not the coach, should supply the discipline.

Lewis was supposed to go to Orange Coast College, but before he even entered the school he decided he was being put down by a coach. He had tried rowing a single the sum-

mer before college to be in top condition. When the freshman coach had spied him at the dock and asked him what
he was doing, Lewis had explained that he was training to
make the junior-varsity boat as a freshman. "There's no way
you're going to do that," the coach had said. "Well, I'd like
to try, anyway," Lewis had said. "There's no way," the
coach had said. "Just forget it." With that, Lewis had put
the shell away and immediately transferred to Cal Irvine. An
era of good crews at Irvine was ending just as he arrived, and
by his senior year he was convinced that there was simply
not enough material for an outstanding eight. He suggested
to the coach that instead of putting together an eight they
concentrate on racing a four, where they could be competitive. That idea was not accepted. Because he was tired of
losing in races where he did not have a chance, he quit and
spent the rest of the year playing volleyball.

Bob Ernst, who had recruited him for Cal Irvine and who
was his first coach there, had taken Brad Lewis's measure
immediately and had decided that he was someone who was
always going to be more interested in individual than in
team sports. His goals would always be personal. There was
with him from the start, Ernst sensed, a wariness that partic-
ipating with others might dilute his own excellence. Ernst
realized that Lewis was an unusual athlete, one who would
train at a very high level and who brought a high degree of
intelligence to everything he did; no one would read more
about sports and about training, and no one would work
harder once he made up his mind about a regimen. But he
was also remarkably immune to most of the forces that motivated college athletes. If a teammate started talking before
a regatta about what they needed to do, trying to motivate
the others, Lewis's withdrawal was self-evident. He seemed
to disappear from the room. Yet Ernst also knew that if he
pushed Brad in a way Brad did not want to be pushed, there
would not be a confrontation. Rather, he would walk away
and never show up again. That made it very hard on many
of his teammates.

Bruce Ibbetson, who rowed and who fought and argued with Lewis during their college years, thought him consummately selfish. The team-oriented Ibbetson could never understand Lewis's more egocentric vision. One source of friction between them was Lewis's willingness to do only what interested him. That did not include much of the menial work involved in rowing, such as taking care of the boats and the boathouse. Lewis was also different from other superior rowers Ibbetson had known in the way in which he chose which days he felt like working hard and which days he did not. On days when he did not want to work hard, he would coast through a piece ("flick it in," the rowers called it). At other times, he might quietly work out alone, build himself up to a certain level; and only when he was sure he could win a practice piece, would he row hard in practice against another sculler. Lewis did not so much compete against the other rower as attack him with a special violence. To Ibbetson that was predatory behavior of the worst kind.

In 1980, he had turned on Lewis all the resentment built up in past years and told him, "You're a shark, nothing but a goddamn shark." The remark did not bother Lewis. It might be that Ibbetson was right. Years later, when Lewis arrived for the single trials in Princeton, he had taped a small rubber shark to his riggings. If his teammates were always wondering why he wasn't like the rest of them, the answers were first that he couldn't be and second that he didn't want to be. Ernst, more aware of that than anyone else was, knew the perfect aspect of rowing for Brad. In Lewis's freshman year, Ernst had started him in a single scull. He had loved it from the start; he was on his own, with no laws or commands to obey save his own.

Lewis believed that if there was any difference between himself and the eastern rowers, it was that they might have accumulated enough racing experience to be mentally tougher. They could be behind in a race by a length and not panic because many times, as collegiate oarsmen, they had been behind and still won. But for someone who came out of a losing program, being behind was a natural state; if you fell behind, you either panicked or you expected to stay there. Tiff Wood had had that toughness built into him when he was seventeen or eighteen. Now, at twenty-nine, Lewis was still trying to learn it, and Tiff Wood was his role model. A photo of the famed Rude and Smooth crew, blown up poster size and hanging outside Harry Parker's office in the Harvard boathouse, fascinated Lewis. To him it was not a photo of eight men but a photo of only one, Tiff Wood, hair shaggy, dark glasses on. Wood might be slightly out of synch with the others and his head might be completely out of position, but looking at him, Lewis saw an image of such intense concentration and such violent physical exertion that his eyes never moved on to the others.

He was so sure that he was now Wood's chief rival that he had turned down the invitation to come to Cambridge to practice with the other scullers. He saw no benefit in going. He was already getting more time on the water than anyone else; and he was receiving very good coaching from Mike Livingston, whom he had come to trust. Livingston was a cultural hybrid, a California boy who had gone to Harvard and rowed on championship crews, including the 1972 Olympic crew, which had won a silver medal at Munich. He had done exceptionally well in college, had gone on to law school and had for a time been a lawyer for the American Civil Liberties Union in the Pacific Northeast before turning to coaching in the late 1970s at Cal Berkeley. The analytical side of him was the Harvard-educated lawyer committed to causes that were not always popular. But the side of him that was the child of California and the 1960s was fascinated with the unknown limits of human experience, the secrets of the mind. A devotee of the writings of Carlos Castaneda, Livingston was convinced that a knowledge of Eastern religion and the study of Yoga could help an athlete to focus and control his or her latent physical powers. At Berkeley he had searched for ways to blend the two experiences together, the rational and the secret sources of strength. He had shared an office with Nort Thornton, the Cal Berkeley swimming coach, who also believed that coaches were fast approaching the outer limits of what they could teach their athletes in terms of strength, endurance and technique. The real frontier in coaching, Thornton believed, was in the area of mental training.

Sports psychology was already a burgeoning field, and it was likely to become even more important in the future. The victory that Livingston sought was over the inner self, an attempt to bring an athlete to his oneness. To that end he tried to create what he described as "white-hot concentration." Crucial to his teachings was what Castaneda taught, the idea of maximizing each moment, or living each day as if it were the last. This was essential not so much for race days, which were already heightened experiences, but for practices, which were usually routine and humdrum. If the athlete was immeasurably toughened in practice, mental toughness on the day of a race would become second nature.

After coaching successfully at Cal Berkeley for three years, Livingston had grown restless and by 1983 was living in Hawaii. During the past year, he had regularly flown back to Newport to coach a group of older men known as the Dirty Dozen who had never rowed before but who were going to make an Olympic challenge in the sweeps. In Newport, he had met Brad Lewis. If Lewis had been suspicious of his past coaches, Livingston was precisely the coach he had been looking for. Livingston was a volunteer, he did not intrude, he did not seek to change anything but rather to reinforce much of what Lewis was already doing. The best thing about him was that he believed in Brad Lewis's abilities and his chance to do well in the single trials.

It was Livingston borrowing from Castaneda, who taught Lewis that the athlete became a warrior. By that he meant a warrior who wins a battle over his inner self, not a samurai warrior, who goes off to fight with others. Lewis seized on the idea, though in his mind the warrior became more of a samurai, a man on a mission of vengeance. Livingston, for his part, was impressed by what Lewis was doing. On his own, Lewis had put together a highly original and exceptionally complete work program. To Livingston, what had kept Lewis going all those years with so little outside support was the idea of improvement as an end in itself. Because he was so dedicated, he had always improved, and because he was always improving, he loved the sport as an index of self-measurement. When Lewis began to ask Livingston for more help, it was Livingston who was cautious. "Brad," he told him, "one of the most powerful aspects of everything you've done is that you've taken complete responsibility for your own workouts and your entire program. Don't lose confidence now. You've been more right about it than you think."

In addition to toughening his mind, in the past year and a half Lewis had worked particularly hard to build up his strength. His cousin Mitch, who had competed at a high level as a weight lifter, was working in Glendora, California, as a therapist and trainer, teaching weight lifting to other athletes. Among his pupils were some members of the Olympic judo team and some track and field athletes. Some rowers shied away from the weight room because of a belief that lifting weights made you musclebound. Oarsmen were supposed to be lean and quick and powerful; they should not look like the Incredible Hulk. Mitch Lewis disagreed; according to him, it was possible to design a weight program that added strength without sacrificing quickness. The Soviets and East Germans were doing this with their oarsmen. It was nonsense to think that greater strength did not allow a rower to exert more pressure on the oar; and if he exerted more pressure, the boat would move faster. Since Brad Lewis saw lack of strength as his only flaw, he had been amenable to working out with his cousin. They would have roughly a year and a half before the Olympics.

Realizing that the weight room was boring for most non-lifters, Mitch Lewis devised a program that would aim for small increments of progress readily achieved, so that Brad would have a tangible sense of accomplishment. The program was also designed to produce results in Brad's rowing as quickly as possible. So three times a week, Brad Lewis had given up his afternoon rowing and worked out with his cousin. In the process, Brad had taken a body that was already big and powerful and made it more so. Within two months, his times for rowing around Lido Island began to drop. One day in October, he called his cousin up. "My God, Mitch," he said, "I cut 23 seconds off my best time for Double Lido today." Brad was hooked; from then on it was easy to keep him working in the weight room.

He had been big, six-four and 190 pounds, and now he had added ten pounds, all in his arms and shoulders. He had done three basic lifts: the squat lift, the dead lift and the bench press. He had gotten up to 315 pounds on the squat lift, 405 on the dead lift and 260 on the bench press. In the world of weight lifting those might be little more than good numbers for a beginner, but for a rower they were impressive; and if that strength could be employed in rowing, there was no question he had improved himself over the past year. (One day at the sculling camp in Hanover, John Biglow had walked in on him while he was working on the bench press. Biglow had tried his hand at 135 pounds, which was the weight Lewis was working on. After struggling through two repetitions, Biglow had quickly gotten out of there. Lewis did not have the heart to tell Biglow that those were the weights he warmed up on, not the ones he exercised with.)

The Princeton weekend was expensive for Lewis. His total expenditure came to nearly $4,000. There was the cost of shipping his shell to the East Coast; and there was the cost of air tickets for him and his cousin Mitch. He also paid Mitch $600 for the time he was missing from his job. Mitch was along to help coach him and to give him body rubs during the heats. That, Brad knew, would be an immense advantage since it would allow his body to come back more quickly after a race than his competitors' could.

CHAPTER
TWELVE

There were no surprises in the heats. Tiff Wood, rowing easily and comfortably, posted the best time, 7:04.1. It was important for him to row the best time; anything less was a sign of vulnerability. Biglow's time was the second best, 7:06.43, and Bouscaren's the third, 7:08.02. Brad Lewis won his heat, and Jim Dietz had come in second in his, 7 seconds behind Biglow. He would have to go to the reps. That did not bother him too much. He had rowed relatively easily and indeed he would survive the reps.

When Tiff Wood saw the draw for the semifinals, he became enraged. The draw was pure chance, but almost all the power was in one heat—he, Biglow, Bouscaren, and Dietz, of whom only three would survive. That meant that no one would be able to coast. Three top contenders in a semi was easy; they could set their pace and stay leisurely ahead of the fourth man. Now that luxury was gone. To make matters worse, the top oarsmen in the other semi would be able to conserve their energy and come out of their heat more rested. (Wood was right; the fourth man in his heat was four seconds under the winning time of the other heat.) Like Wood, Jim Dietz knew exactly what the draw for the semifinals meant: To make the finals, he would have to go all out in the semi. His plan to sneak in and row one great surprise race was dead.

By contrast, Brad Lewis's confidence grew even stronger. He had sat there and listened while the officials had called off the names of the oarsmen in the first semifinal: Bouscaren, Biglow, Dietz, Wood. He had waited for his name, and when they had not read it, he had heaved a sigh of relief. The other four were going to kill each other in their semi, while he was going to be so able to coast in his that he did not even intend to win it.

The semifinal heat was very tight and very well rowed. Wood won, Biglow was a close second and Bouscaren and Dietz were in a virtual dead heat for third. Dietz had surprised everyone. Usually he was almost as fast off the mark as an eight, but this time he had conserved his energy, held back and unleashed a furious closing drive. He had pushed Bouscaren so hard that Wood, who was keying on Bouscaren, had been forced to give a hard ten with about thirty strokes to go. That had made Wood the winner. Dietz was sure he had beaten Bouscaren. His friends were sure of it. Most of the other rowers thought he had won. Yet it was called a dead heat. Dietz was furious. He was sure that Harry Parker, whom he considered an old nemesis, was behind it. He demanded to see the videotape, but the videotape, because the camera was at too low an angle, showed nothing conclusive. Another rower had blocked out the finish between the two boats, and both were allowed to qualify.

The decision did not please Wood. Bouscaren was his friend in a loose definition of the term, but it was an odd and wary friendship, based only on their competition. If Wood and Biglow used their mutual love of the sport to bind themselves into an unlikely but genuine friendship, Wood and Bouscaren grated on each other. The semifinal had been a hard race for almost everyone. Dietz had been forced to use up the energy he wanted to save for the final, and there was a possibility that Tiff Wood had, too. At the end, Wood had turned to Biglow and said, "good race." The words had pleased Biglow, for they indicated that Wood had been forced to push himself, which might be an advantage. If an event was about pure boat speed, it aided Wood; if it was about endurance—and two hard races were an endurance test—it might favor Biglow.

No one, at least no one in America, could come from behind against Biglow, and few could hold him off at the end. Tiff Wood was powerful enough to hold off Biglow if he had a length lead at the start of the last five hundred meters. But even that would be shaved very close. The race was two thousand meters, and the final five hundred meters lasted about 1:50 minutes. Tiff Wood could sprint at the end, but he could not sprint the entire 500 meters the way Biglow could.

The reason for this was physiological. There are two kinds of muscles for athletes: slow twitch and fast twitch. Slow-twitch muscles allow an athlete to replenish himself and are ideal for sports that demand great endurance. These same athletes usually have trouble generating quick, early bursts of speed. Fast-twitch muscles generate speed very quickly but often cannot replenish their energy. a tissue cut of John Biglow's body revealed that 72 percent of his muscles were slow twitch, while Wood's count was in the low sixties. Harry Parker believed that Joe Bouscaren's count (Bouscaren had never had the biopsy) was a good deal less. Therefore, Joe, the most elegant oar of the three, was the rabbit of the group. He could generate power more quickly than the others, but he tended to burn out at the end.

Joe Bouscaren had thought about the final for a long time and had carefully planned his race. He would go out early, but not so fast that he would burn himself out. The semifinal had been as hard on him as on the others. The challenge by Dietz at the end had caught him by surprise, and Bouscaren had been forced to give everything he had. He was aware that he had almost missed the cut and that Dietz's friends were saying that Harry had lobbied for him.

Of all the oarsmen in the final, John Biglow tended to be

the most consistent and the most secure. He always rowed his own race, and if someone else went out too quickly at the start, Biglow did not change his game plan. What he did in each five-hundred-meter piece was very much like what he did in all the other five-hundred-meter pieces. He had felt increasingly confident going into the final. In the semifinal, he had started out poorly. He had been off balance on the first stroke, and because the first stroke had been poor, it had taken him several strokes to settle down. In the immense anxiety created by the idea of the race, he thought of giving up and not rowing at all. He had had the same feeling in the past and had recognized it as a form of anxiety attack. That anxiety came, he knew, from the pain, as if his body were trying to get him to quit. For a moment he had felt himself think, I simply will not row hard today because I don't feel like racing. It was a form of instant terror to which he had never given in. He gradually settled down and he had rowed well in the semifinal. What pleased him at the end was his sense that race by race he was rowing more strongly.

In the final he intended to work off Tiff Wood. If Biglow could stay within a length of Tiff at the five-hundred mark, he was confident he could win.

Because the wind kept rising above acceptable levels, the officials had to delay the start of the final. Tiff Wood sat on the lakebank in his Saab, his fiancée and his family coming over to talk to him and then quickly departing. His mood did not encourage small talk. He seemed a part of this event and this party yet completely distant from it. There was too much time to think. Even fighting off tension was a sign that the tension was considerable. He liked, as much as any sculler could, the act of racing, but in the past he had been plagued by his own doubts. He was certain of his physical abilities and his willingness to pay whatever price the race demanded, but he was aware that before a race he often became too tight and constricted, too emotionally involved in what was yet to take place, for his own good. He envied John Biglow's confidence. Confidence it might not really be, but it *seemed* like confidence, and that was good enough. Biglow was going around the area where everyone was waiting, appearing hardly mindful of the event just ahead.

Only in 1983 had Wood been miraculously able to free himself from the tension that plagued him. That had been a wonderful year for him. Beaten by Biglow in 1981, Wood had rededicated himself to rowing in 1982, working hard for the first time on his technique. His major fault had been that, in rowing terms, he "shot his slide"—that is, he did not connect the drive of his legs and the drive of the rest of his body well, a failing that not only cost him power but also made the boat lurch. The hard work he poured into rowing in 1982 was beginning to show dividends near the latter part of the season, and he had been optimistic about the 1982 trials. Then, in the final in 1982, he had had to row on an appalling course in Camden, New Jersey. It was poorly marked, and he had hit several buoys in succession; he hit the last one hard and flipped. He had been in the process of saying "oh, shit" when he landed in the water. He had wanted the race rerowed, and the Olympic officials who were there had agreed, but the local people had been unwilling to do it. That had ended his hopes for 1982.

But the hard work he had put in had paid off the next year, when things that had never gone right suddenly started falling into place, both in his rowing and in his personal life. It was if he were touched, floating above himself. That feeling had carried right through from the American trials to the world championship at Duisburg in West Germany.

Pertti Karppinen, the great Finnish champion, was not rowing singles in 1983. Peter-Michael Kolbe of West Germany; Uwe Mund of East Germany; and Vassily Yakusha of the Soviet Union, the silver medalist from the Moscow Olympics, were favored to finish in that order. Looking at the field, Tiff Wood suddenly had a strong feeling that he could medal. He was there, he kept reminding himself, because he was *the best sculler in the United States of America*. He was already a champion; no one had a right to demand anything more of him. In that sense he was in the perfect position to do well; little was expected of him, and he felt immensely confident. In his heat against Kolbe, who was probably the second-best sculler in the world, Wood had rowed almost even, losing by one second. That had placed him in the repechage. He easily made the semifinal, and though he did not row particularly well in the semi, he still came in second to Mund, with Yakusha third. Wood had scrambled from the start, rowing clumsily and heavily, exerting far too much energy for the speed he was generating. Even so, he had beaten Yakusha. Kolbe and Mund might be a level above him, but they were within reach on the right day. Never had he felt so optimistic.

When the final started, Kolbe, Mund and Yakusha all went out quickly, far ahead of him. After the first hundred meters, he could not even see them. He felt an immediate disappointment and faulted himself for his foolish vanity. He would have to be content with simply rowing his own best race. It would not be the worst thing to come in fourth or fifth. At 250 meters he took a power ten to try to make even the smallest move on one of the three leading boats. It was a futile effort; they were all still out of sight. At that point, he had to fight against losing his desire and his mental toughness. The one thing that kept him going was a sense that he was rowing well. At the thousand-meter mark he still could not see the three leaders. Then, with five hundred meters to go, he looked and, miraculously, there was Yakusha very near him; the two of them were in a real race. If he had fallen that far back, Wood knew, Yakusha was in real trouble. So Wood poured it on, summoning every bit of energy he could, gaining not just on Yakusha but on Kolbe as well. The Soviet was burned. With barely fifty strokes left in the race, Wood heard the crowd; the roar was enormous and it was not for Kolbe. Rather it was a West German crowd cheering for an unheralded American who was going to beat a Soviet. With thirty strokes to go, Wood passed Yakusha. I'm going to get a medal, he thought, I'm going to get a world medal. Suddenly he panicked; and thinking he had made a mistake, he quickly counted the number of boats that had finished and the number still on the water. He had not miscounted; he was third. He was the bronze medalist. He had beaten the man who had been second in Moscow. It was for Wood a glorious and lasting moment, and he still found it remarkably easy to hear that West German crowd cheering him on.

A few weeks later he had rowed at Lake Casitas near Santa Barbara in a regatta that had been specially scheduled as a pre-Olympic tune-up so that American and foreign oarsmen and coaches could test the water there. Though Kolbe and Karppinen did not show, the field was fast—Ricardo Ibarra of Argentina, Svensson of Sweden, Mund of East Germany, Pat Walter of Canada and John Biglow. Wood had rowed very well in the final; Mund and Ibarra had gone out early on him, but he had rowed through Mund at 750 meters and then, with ease, through Ibarra at fifteen hundred meters, winning with energy to burn. Biglow had taken fourth. The race confirmed that Duisburg was not a fluke. But a few months later, both victories were something of a burden to Wood, for in 1984, all the American scullers were tracking him. As the favorite, he was everybody's target.

The crowd at Princeton was small, more like an expanded tailgate party than an Olympic qualifying event. Most of the hundred or so people watching the semifinals were other rowers, or friends or families of oarsmen. Some doubles races were also taking place, scheduled by Kris Korzeniowski, the sweep coach, as part of the sweep selection. John Biglow's present roommate, Fred Borchelt, was rowing in a pair, as was Steve Kiesling.

On the sidelines the families of several of the oarsmen were grouped, old friends now at a reunion. Anthony Bouscaren, Joe's father, congratulated Richard Wood, Tiff's father, on how well Tiff had rowed this year, and John Biglow came over to talk with the fathers of his two chief adversaries. He knew Anthony Bouscaren very well, since Mr. Bouscaren had watched John almost as faithfully as he had watched his own son during their Yale years. Biglow had also, from more recent sculling championships, come to know Richard Wood; and he told Mr. Wood that his own father, Lucius Biglow, a passionate follower and photographer of his son's rowing activities, had taken some great shots of Mr. Wood and Tiff at last year's world finals. The fact that Mr. Biglow was not present at this race was taken by some of Biglow's competitors as a sign that John's back still was not completely healed; they were sure Mr. Biglow would not miss an Olympic trial if John was truly ready.

All of this managed to give the impression of an event from another time and another place as yet uninterrupted by change. It was probably the absence of television as much as anything that allowed the past to survive and remain so powerful. Since ABC was handling the Olympics, it was duty bound to include rowing. There had been talk about one of the scullers going on *Good Morning, America* to appear with a veteran sculler of the past, perhaps Dr. Benjamin Spock, but the people from *GMA* had wanted to tape the show in advance of the race. Dr. Spock, said Kathryn Reith, the young press officer from the U.S. Rowing Association, with a small measure of disdain, may have been a gold medalist, but he had rowed *sweeps,* not sculled in the 1924 Olympics. It was not, she said, the same sport. Well, said the *GMA* people, perhaps she could come up with an old-time sculler and the winner for the single sculls in time for their deadline. "We cannot," said Ms. Reith, "tell you the name of the winner, since we have not held the finals yet." The idea, not surprisingly, was soon abandoned.

Tiff Wood working out in a single

Joe Bouscaren starting a workout on the Charles

John Biglow before a practice

JOSEF SCALYEA, Seattle *Times*

A pre-Olympic workout in a quad. Stroking: John Biglow, Paul Enquist, Brad Lewis and Tiff Wood

Henley 1977. Gregg Stone and Tiff Wood in a double

Tiff Wood getting a world bronze at Duisburg in 1983

Harry Parker, coaching on the Charles

Tiff Wood showing with the violence of his stroke
why he was called The Hammer

Brad Lewis as a young sculler in 1976

John Biglow, smaller than his two German opponents,
gets a world bronze in 1981. From left, Rudiger
Reiche, who got the silver, Peter-Michael Kolbe, who
got the gold.

Paul Enquist (left) and Brad Lewis celebrate their
Olympic victory.

CHAPTER
THIRTEEN

Tiff Wood took fifteen strokes in the final and knew he was rowing the wrong race, not setting his own pace, unable to take command. It was almost, he said later, as if he had been in some way predisposed toward defeat. Within a minute, he had the terrible sense he was going to lose. He did not think it was fatigue from the previous race; it seemed more mental. Perhaps he had been too aware of Biglow's advantage in back-to-back hard races. There was, he decided later, a softness to his rowing, as if he were rowing in a fog. He had had races like that before, when things moved as if beyond his control, but he had never had them happen at such a critical moment.

In the final, Joe Bouscaren went out much faster than he intended to. At the five-hundred-meter mark he had a half length on Tiff Wood and open water on the rest of the field. Bouscaren felt fast and strong. He was sure he was rowing not just well, but also his best. Then, suddenly, around the twelve-hundred-meter mark, Brad Lewis had surged ahead, going by so quickly that Bouscaren could not even respond. That seemed to stagger him mentally for a moment, and he felt a letdown. He had not expected Brad to make so quick a surge. Now as he looked out he saw both Wood and Biglow beginning their sprints. It was hard for him to find more energy, and he had a sense that he had gone out too fast.

Brad Lewis, who expected Bouscaren to go out early, had decided to pace himself and to burn off as little energy as possible in the first thousand meters. Two or three years ago endurance had been a problem for him, and he knew the Easterners expected him to tire. Now he was sure that he knew how to race. That was not easy. It took a long time to learn how to plan your race, ration your energy, understand the strengths and weaknesses of your opponents, not to panic if someone else went out too quickly. At the halfway mark Lewis was surprised by how easy the race seemed. Suddenly, knowing the others were not expecting him to, he took his shell out. His surge, coming just when they expected him to fade, caught them completely by surprise. He had a full length on the others before they knew what had happened. He felt absolutely wonderful. The race was going just as he had envisioned during all those weeks alone in California.

That Bouscaren had gone out quickly and taken the early lead did not bother Biglow. What threw him off was Tiff Wood's slow start. It was unlike Tiff to come out so slowly; Tiff was a rower who liked to take charge of a race. Biglow thought Wood was up to some new strategy, decoying him and trying to throw him off. Why is Tiff hanging back? he thought—if I had the ability to generate speed and power the way he does, I'd be out as far in front as I could. With that he decided to go ahead and row his own race. At about the midway point of the race Biglow passed Sean Colgan, another sculler, and Jim Dietz. Only then did Biglow notice to his astonishment that Brad Lewis was moving out on Bouscaren, and in fact moving out very strongly. Although Lewis was a good sculler and a desperately serious one, he had not been part of Biglow's calculations for this race. Now here Lewis was, rowing more strongly than ever at just the point where he usually began to fade. Clearly Brad Lewis had improved a great deal in the past year without anyone noticing it. Looking at the two lengths of open water between him and Lewis, Biglow thought two lengths was too big a lead for the final five-hundred; it would take nothing but sheer pain to catch Brad, assuming he could be caught.

But it seemed wrong to Biglow that Brad Lewis should be the sculler. It offended his Biglovian sense of order and hierarchy. It was easy to picture Tiff as the single sculler. He was intelligent and confident, he was very good at handling the media and he was an exceptional spokesman for the rowers. But Brad Lewis was different. He looks confident, Biglow thought, and he talks confidently, but the confidence does not seem genuine. It comes and goes, just as he is friendly with the other oarsmen and then unfriendly. John Biglow decided he did not like the image of Brad Lewis as the single sculler. With five-hundred meters to go, Biglow set out to catch him. Probably Biglow would have tried to win anyway, but his feelings about Lewis gave him more reason. Slowly and steadily he closed on the leader, still sure that the lead was too great.

At this point, Tiff Wood, too, realized that Brad Lewis, whom he had always beaten, was ahead. When it looked like Brad was going to win, Tiff began to push himself harder. He felt the boat begin to move faster. Wood began to come on strongly, passing one shell after another. He was surging, gaining on Lewis, but Biglow was surging, too, and Wood knew that it was going to be very hard to catch both of them. He might have caught Lewis and at the end he had been gaining on Biglow. If there had been another hundred meters he might have won. If, he thought in his anger, *if* . . .

Brad Lewis saw Biglow make his move. His boat seemed to jump out of the water in what was obviously going to be one of those special Biglow sprints. Lewis was far from tiring. If anything, he felt relatively strong. It was simply that Biglow at this point in a race was awe-inspiring. Lewis decided that all he could do was to remain calm and count in sets of tens. Five hundred meters meant six sets of tens. The finish line was coming up and Biglow, and now Tiff Wood, were charging at him, with Wood coming on even faster.

As they neared the finish line, John Biglow had a sense that Brad Lewis was coming back on him. Was Lewis coasting because he was so much in control and the finish line so near? That was a possibility, but the other possibility was that he was falling just short and dying right there. Biglow reached back and poured on everything he had. He saw Tiff Wood making his charge. With thirty strokes left, Biglow heard people on the shore chanting, and he thought they were shouting, "Biggy! Biggy!" If they were rooting for him, he still had a chance. That gave him another boost, and he poured everything into the last thirty strokes. He knew, as he crossed the finish line, that he had closed on Brad, but he was sure that Lewis had won. It was as close a race as Biglow could remember. The only thing that gave him hope was that perhaps he had looked at the finish from a bad angle. Earlier in the weekend, when he had rowed the course with Bouscaren, Joe had showed him the finish line and had told him that it was an odd one. There was an optical illusion at the end, and the man who wins may be the loser. Even though he saw Tony Johnson, his old Yale coach, give him a thumbs-up sign, he was not sure he had won.

The judges decided that Biglow had won in 7:27.1, that Lewis was second in 7:28, that Wood was third with 7:28.1 and Bouscaren fourth with 7:32.1. Jim Dietz, burned out by two hard back-to-back races, had come in seventh.

Lewis was not happy. He had come so close, only to see victory slip away. Besides, he did not entirely accept the decision of the judges. Who knew whether they had the right angle, or whether they could see accurately something as close as that final? He had beaten Tiff, he had almost rowed the race he had intended and somehow Biglow had probably slipped by. Everyone else was stunned by how well he had rowed, but he was bitterly disappointed. "We did everything right," he told Mitch Lewis that night. "The only thing wrong was that I didn't win." All he wanted to do was get away from the scullers and away from Princeton.

Tiff Wood went over and congratulated Biglow, who seemed puzzled by Wood's race. When he asked Tiff why had been so slow off the line, it was not a question Wood could answer. Instead, he put his arm around Biglow and said, "John, the thing I'll miss most about your winning is that now we won't be able to row the double together." Then Tiff Wood joined his family for a tailgate picnic. He felt terrible to have invested so much for so long and then to have rowed so badly. The worst thing of all was that he had had energy left at the end. That was almost sinful.

He would probably row in the Olympics in a double or a quad, *but not the single*, the goal he had sought with such determination for so long. He kept his disappointment in and tried to enjoy the picnic before driving home with Kristy. She was in tears, taking his loss even harder than he did. He did not talk about the race very much, but she knew he was rerowing it all the way home. What he wanted to do was scream. Instead, every once in a while he would simply say, "oh, shit." It was a very long ride back from Princeton.

FOURTEEN

John Biglow did not return to Cambridge immediately. Instead, he drove to Connecticut to spend a few days with Grandmother Biglow. He had wanted to share the pleasure of his triumph with her. She was ninety-four and they were not going to be able to have that much more time together. Even though she could get around now only with a walker, Grandmother Biglow was still competitive. She listened faithfully to radio broadcasts of Yale sports events with the Yale programs and alumni magazine in front of her so she would know as much as possible about the players. When a player entered the game, she would say, "Oh, John, he's very good," and she would detail his accomplishments. (A few months later, John Biglow met the Harvard quarterback at a party and said to that young man's astonishment, "Oh, listen, my grandmother thinks you're very good. She's a real fan of yours.")

She had not been in favor of his rowing this year; she thought he had given too much to the sport at the expense of himself and the Biglow family; it was time to go on to other things. He had tried to explain that this year was different, that this was an Olympic year. In the days he spent with her after the trials, the phone rang incessantly with different people calling to congratulate him and interview him. When she asked him what all the fuss was about, he said that it was the *Olympics*, that he had won the right to represent his own country against the world. "Oh," she had said, "that's nice," and she had been pleased and he had known that the Olympics were all right with her.

He was supposed to return to Cambridge on Tuesday. On Monday, he called Harry Parker. They had talked about the race, and in the middle of the conversation Biglow had said, "I have a feeling that you would have preferred that Tiff had won."

Parker was startled. He had become accustomed to dealing with Biglow and his quick flashes of brutal frankness and candor; but this caught him off guard, in no small part because it was true. He realized immediately that he had to match Biglow's candor with his own. "I think you're right, John," he answered. "I think I did prefer that Tiff win because you're almost equal as scullers, and I think you're better in the team boats than he is."

"Do you want me to switch to a double or a quad, and for Tiff to row the single?" Biglow asked.

Parker knew that more than anything else in the world, John Biglow wanted to row the single in the Olympics. This, then, was treacherous water. It was time to call a stop. "John, that question was answered on Sunday. You're the single sculler," Parker said. He was, he thought, dealing with a very unusual man.

FIFTEEN

If the Sunday of the trial had been bad for Tiff Wood, the Monday after the trial was even worse. That was the day the Soviets pulled out of the 1984 Olympics; and Tiff Wood, who was almost never on television in his years of glory, was besieged by local television reporters. He was local, he was an Olympic-level athlete, he was articulate. He did four shows in one afternoon. "Are we getting our just due for 1980?" one of the reporters asked. "As a member of the 1980 team, I think there is all the more reason to let the athletes compete," he answered, "but many of us were afraid something like this would happen. If only the Soviets pull out, this isn't so bad. But if the East Germans, who are the best rowers in the world, stay out, then it makes the games less meaningful."

"Does that mean that a medal will be less sweet?" he was asked.

"Medals are always sweet," he answered.

"Will this cut down on the fans coming to see you?" another reporter asked.

"No one comes to see the rowing, anyway," he replied.

The next day he joined Biglow at the boathouse. Biglow was wearing a Soviet rowing jacket and a Soviet rowing hat in protest. He was angry.

It was like being cheated, he said. He did not care very much about the Soviets, but the withdrawal of the East Germans mattered. He had rowed against Rudiger Reiche of East Germany, whom he liked even though Reiche was not allowed to talk to him. The East Germans frowned on fraternization. But Reiche was cool and graceful, and he would wink at Biglow. The wink seemed to say, "Listen, a lot of this is crap, but being an athlete, doing what we do at this level, is something special, and we have this together. I know about you and you know about me, and that is enough. We are connected."

The failure of the Soviets and the Eastern Bloc nations to attend the Olympics did not dramatically change the projected order of finish for the singles. The medal the American scullers were most likely to win remained a bronze, for Biglow, at Lake Casitas near Santa Barbara, California, would be rowing against two of the greatest scullers of all time, Pertti Karppinen of Finland and Peter-Michael Kolbe of West Germany. Karppinen, who had won the gold in 1976 and 1980, was probably the greatest sculler of all time, greater even than the legendary three-time gold medalist Vasily Ivanov of the Soviet Union. Kolbe, in any other era, might also have three golds.

Karppinen was a Ruthian figure, someone so far above the others that he turned his event into a sport of his own. To Biglow, Karppinen was a god. One did not even think of beating him. One hoped, instead, that a fever still worked in Kolbe's brain so that he would make one last mad attempt to beat Karppinen, burn out and leave an unlikely chance for the silver. For Biglow, just to be in a race with Karppinen was a privilege.

Karppinen was six-seven and weighed about 220 pounds. His upper body was massive, and his shoulders and his chest might have been forged by a demented left-wing sculptor who wanted to project the idea of what a people's worker truly looked like. Yet he was surprisingly supple. That a man that big and strong could compete in so small and delicate a boat was extraordinary. The scull was only twelve inches across, and even the slightest mistake or shift of weight could flip it. Karppinen was the perfectly cast Scandinavian country boy, big, powerful, uncorrupted by modern ways. The son of a stonecutter in the small town of Vehmaa on the eastern coast of Finland, he was one of six children. When, in 1976, he had won the first of his gold medals, most of the local villagers had made a pilgrimage to the Karppinen home to offer their congratulations; the congratulations had to be offered personally because the Karppinens did not own a phone.

Karppinen had started sculling as a boy, and by 1974, at twenty-one, he was sculling seriously. At first he was big and awkward and weak, and he tended to fall behind near the end. At Montreal, in 1976, Kolbe, a *Wunderkind* of sculling, a world champion at the age of nineteen, was the heavy favorite. He was six-four, powerful, already skilled in his technique. In the single-scull final, he had gone out quickly, and at a thousand meters he had held a commanding lead. Karppinen, then virtually unknown, was 8 seconds behind him, a seemingly insurmountable time lag. Then Karppinen started his sprint. The finish was one of the most dramatic in Olympic history. With two hundred meters to go, Kolbe still looked unbeatable, but he was beginning to fade. Karppinen was rowing with a fury. With fifty meters to go, Kolbe was still ahead. With fifteen meters left, Karppinen passed him to win by 2.5 seconds. In 1980, Karppinen won another gold, at Moscow, and Kolbe, observing the American boycott, did not compete. Now, if the predictions were accurate, Karppinen would get his third gold at Casitas; Kolbe, his second silver; and John Biglow would have a good chance at a bronze.

John Biglow left the camp in Hanover early to row in Europe in a series of lesser races before a major regatta at Lucerne, which, in turn, was the final tune-up for the Olympics. He did not row well in Europe and quickly became frustrated with himself. His back was better, but something was wrong.

What was most upsetting was that he was not rowing as well as he had when he had first come on the international rowing scene three years earlier, at the age of twenty-three. The first international final in which he had competed had been only the seventh race of his sculling career, and his first heat at Munich had been only his fifth singles race. Yet he had done amazingly well. The summer of 1981 still had a dreamlike quality for him. He had expected that the ascent to the American title would be a slow one, and instead he had won the sculling trial in his first year. Then the national team had gone to Munich for the world championship. Harry Parker was the coach, and one day he had told Biglow, "Except for Kolbe, I'm not sure there's anyone here you can't beat." (Karppinen was rowing a double that year, staying out of the singles competition.) Biglow, listening to Parker, thought his voice was off, that Harry did not believe his own words. He thinks I have an outside chance at fifth, Biglow decided. In his world-championship heat he rowed against Ricardo Ibarra of Argentina, who had just won the Henley singles and who Biglow's old coach, Frank Cunningham, thought a magnificent oarsman. But Biglow, too young and inexperienced to be scared, passed Ibarra with five hundred meters to go. Although he waited for the expected resurgence from Ibarra, Ibarra had not surged, and Biglow simply widened his margin of victory.

Not only had Biglow, to his surprise, won the heat, but he had also turned in the fastest qualifying time. It can't be this easy, he thought. In the semifinal behind Kolbe of West Germany, who was the favorite, he had taken third. That had been his only nervous moment because his own goal had been to make the final, which meant he had to do well in the semi.

In the final he had felt particularly free. I have nothing to lose, he thought, because I don't even belong here. He had rowed against Kolbe and Rudiger Reiche, and they had gone out far ahead of him. But he had rowed his own race, and he had won the bronze at the age of twenty-three. Harry Parker had been at the finish line, smiling in a way Biglow had never seen him smile and clicking away with his camera, taking hundreds of photos. Could what happened be that important to Harry? Biglow wondered. At the end he had felt like crying; he had achieved everything he had wanted and had medaled in a world regatta in just one year. He remembered standing on the platform with Kolbe and Reiche and thinking, I am with two of the greatest rowers in the world. I am the bronze.

He had spent the rest of the day practicing the ancient trade of international oarsmen, bartering uniforms with other rowers. He had come away with a good Swiss sweat suit (less exotic than a Soviet suit, which he already owned, but of better quality) and a West German rowing shirt. That night his friends were going out on the town, but all he wanted to do was fall asleep. His celebration, fittingly enough, was within himself, just as his discovery was of himself. Up until that day he had always played with the idea of going to medical school. He had taken some premed courses and had not done particularly well in them. As such his self-doubts had won out and he had held back from committing himself to medical school. But now, having accomplished this, he felt there was nothing he could not achieve. He decided to go back to school, take more premed courses and aim for medicine.

In 1982 he had returned, more confident and more ambitious. Neither Kolbe nor Karppinen was rowing, but Reiche, at six-five and 200 pounds, was virtually the equal of Kolbe. In the first heat, Biglow had rowed against Reiche. Believing (erroneously) that only one man would qualify for the semifinals, he had pushed himself hard. It had been a very strong race. Biglow was racing hard because he thought he had to win, and Reiche was racing hard because he liked to race. Reiche won by .1 second. Biglow later learned that at the end of the race Reiche had turned to his coach and asked, "Well, what do we do now?"

Biglow believed he could win the final. He concentrated on Reiche and paid little attention to Yakusha of the Soviet Union, whom he had beaten earlier. Reiche and Yakusha had gone out early, but with 750 meters left, Biglow had started sprinting. In the last five hundred meters he had a quarter length on Yakusha. Then the Soviet sprinted hard himself and moved past Biglow. It was the first time anyone had rowed through John Biglow in a single scull near the end of a race. Biglow had his second bronze, 1.41 seconds behind Reiche. This time, he realized, Reiche had been ready for him.

CHAPTER
SIXTEEN

All of that promised even greater achievements in the future.
But Biglow's performances had leveled out. He had been
limited by his back in 1983, and his return to form had been
slower than he had expected. As he prepared for the Olympics, Biglow more and more began to wonder whether he
was concentrating his efforts in the right direction. It was as
if he were caught between two conflicting sets of coaches, his
eastern ones and his western ones, who reflected the schism
in the world of U.S. rowing. His eastern coaches, Harry
Parker and Tony Johnson, were disciples of men such as Joe
Burk in this country and Karl Adam, coach of the famed
Ratzeburg crew in West Germany. When Adam's crew,
made up of basically Ratzeburg oarsmen, had won in the
1960 Olympics, he had become an influential figure in
America. The Ratzeburg rowers had shown that strength
and endurance could take precedence over form. They emphasized endurance training, their oarsmen ran great distances, they lifted weights, they worked on the ergometer
and they rowed on the water to improve their stamina.
Coaches such as Parker and Johnson were innately wary of
tinkering with a young man's form if he was rowing well and
moving boats. "Do it, just do it," Tony Johnson had always
said. "Pull hard and row. Don't think about it." A centipede,

Johnson added, could not walk if it had to think of which leg
came next.

By contrast, Biglow's West Coast coaches were traditionalists who valued form more than power. They were men
such as Frank Cunningham, who had stroked Harvard, and
Charley McIntyre, a successful sculler who had rowed with
his brother in a national-championship double. Their men-
tor was George Pocock, a legendary sculler and boat builder
in the Seattle area. They considered those who favored
power over technique the Philistines of sculling. Power over
technique in an eight sweep was one thing, but not in a scull.
They were convinced that the Europeans' great advantage
in sculling lay in an emphasis on technique. McIntyre chau-
vinistically raged against the American coaches who listened
to Adam, whose teachings they had to translate; Pocock and
his followers not only were better teachers but also had written in English. To Cunningham and McIntyre, Biglow,
more than any other American sculler, was *their* sculler and
their hope. After going East to college, he had strayed from
the true course and been seduced by the theory of power and
endurance. He had gone over to the Easterners and sacrificed style for strength. Not surprisingly, they believed his
rowing had slipped and he had stopped improving.

McIntyre was particularly outspoken on the subject. As
far as he was concerned, Biglow's prowess came from his
being more graceful on the slide than other, stronger racers.
The slide was the moving seat upon which the rower sat, and
it was Biglow's particular skill to be able to apply his power
smoothly without lurching and jerking on the slide. That
made boat movement considerably smoother. "Beat them on
the slide," McIntyre always lectured Biglow. He hated it
when Biglow went for power and abandoned his technique.
"He's chopping wood again," McIntyre would now say,
meaning Biglow was putting too much back into his motion
and losing his rhythm. The previous spring he had written
Biglow a long, angry letter. "Stop! Stop! Stop! Or to hell
with you because you won't listen to me anyway." This

spring, rowing poorly in Europe and watching the excellent performances of the American sweep oarsmen whose coaches emphasized technique, Biglow was not so sure that Cunningham and McIntyre were wrong. Perhaps, he thought, his technique had slipped and it had cost him.

John Biglow had been very well coached as a young man, principally by Frank Cunningham, a onetime Harvard stroke who believed that he understood the western migration of the Biglows, since he had made a comparable one himself. Cunningham had grown up as the son of privileged Easterners, had gone to Harvard and, because of his size, had rowed there on the lightweight crew. His college years had been interrupted by the war. Marine boot camp had been a revelation to him. He had found himself the best-educated man in his unit, yet, in an odd way, the least free. All the other young men were talking about what they were going to do after the war, but Cunningham knew only what his family intended for him to do. He had never thought of determining his own future. The idea of opening up his own business, as some of these young men were planning, was absolutely beyond him. He was a Cunningham, and while Cunninghams were not exactly Cabots or Lodges, they took their obligations equally seriously. For Frank Cunningham, there were too many standards to be met, too many links to the past.

He had returned to Harvard after the war and instead of rowing lights, he had, at only five-ten and 165 pounds, stroked the Harvard heavies to a very good record, including a victory in Seattle in what stood for more than three decades as a record time for a twelve-boat regatta. A year later, still unsure of what he wanted to do and feeling that he was not measuring up to Cunningham standards, he bummed across the country with a friend and ended up in Seattle where, among the relatively small group of Harvard alumni, his rowing exploits still loomed large. In Seattle, unlike the East, there seemed to be much less in the way of expectations. A few weeks after he arrived, he had been at dinner with some Harvard alumni when someone asked him if he had found a job yet. "No," he had answered, "not yet," but he was about to start looking. "There's no rush, Frank," the man had answered, "take your time. Plenty of time." With that Cunningham knew he had finally found a home and a place where he could breathe.

He started out by coaching the junior rowing program for the city of Seattle; then he coached and taught in the public-school system before moving to Lakeside, a model country day school for the children of the upper middle class, as an English teacher and rowing coach. He was an unusual coach. He promised Lakeside a good and disciplined program and that the kids would be off the water at 5:30 P.M. He did not promise victories. He had no intention of being a coach whose ego was mixed up in whether a group of seventeen-year-olds won or lost. As far as victories went, he had had enough victories at Harvard to last a lifetime. He would teach his athletes to row. The rest was up to them. He did not promise them that rowing would be fun. If it was, so much the better. If parents complained about the lack of intensity (and by and large they did not, for Frank Cunningham was a tough man, one whom parents did not lightly criticize, or at least criticize to his face), he would say that the intensity went into keeping the boathouse clean and repairing the boats. But he had been coached by masters, Tom Bolles and Bert Haines at Harvard (Bert Haines was the lightweight coach, and when the young Cunningham had approached him and asked how to row an important race, Haines had answered, "Frank, get ahead at the start and stay ahead."), and he was ready to pass on his knowledge. Whenever someone would ask him how his boats had done in competition, his standard answer—"We lose more than we win"—was almost gleeful. He did not push his people, but the oarsmen who came out of his program were as good as any in the country.

The relationship between Frank Cunningham and John Biglow was complicated. It was filled with admiration, ambiguity, reservations and dramatically different objectives. Cunningham thought Biglow a remarkable oar but wanted him to be more independent and more complete as a person. Biglow, in turn, talked of Cunningham as a coach who was more concerned with technique and taking care of the boathouse than he was about winning. Lakeside was a school where soccer was as important as football and where rowing was a prestige sport. Not the least of the reasons for its prestige was the fact that many parents wanted their children to go to Ivy League schools, and there was no better Ivy League ticket than rowing

In the fall of his first year at Lakeside, John Biglow had played soccer, and during the winter he had played some squash and in the spring he had thought of rowing, mainly because the people who rowed had standing in the school and were socially pleasant. He did not like it his first year; it was serious, hard work, and Cunningham had seemed to him to be too critical. Besides, there was not enough emphasis on winning, which would at least give some sense of reward for all the work invested. He decided not to row in his sophomore year, and Frank Cunningham did not try to change his mind. As far as Cunningham was concerned, each boy knew what was best for himself. In his sophomore year Biglow played lacrosse, which had been his father's sport at Yale. But lacrosse had seemed too rough to him. If it had been more like women's lacrosse, with additional padding and protection, he might have enjoyed it. That spring, while driving home from school, he had stopped for a moment on a floating bridge. The water was calm, and he was delighted by the serenity of the scene beneath him. Just then a crew had rowed by, and Biglow had experienced such a powerful desire to row that he could feel the rowing motion in his body. The sport had given him far more pleasure than he had ever realized.

So in his junior year he once again went out for crew. Biglow had been an exceptional rower as a freshman, and Cunningham was pleased to have him back, keener than ever.

The problem was that the Biglow who returned was, as far as Cunningham was concerned, more of a nuisance than a pleasure. In Cunningham's view, Biglow wanted to intellectualize the sport. He asked endless questions and wanted details and reasons for everything. Some of his curiosity, Cunningham thought, stemmed from deep interest in rowing, and some of it was to set himself apart from the other rowers and gain special attention. There was Biglow constantly asking for explanations, and there was Cunningham telling him, "John, when you do it right, you'll *feel* it." Biglow would again demand an explanation, and Cunningham would say, "Goddamn it, John, just *do* it." Cunningham's irritation came to a head one day in the boathouse when Biglow asked a question about technique.

Cunningham brushed him aside, but Biglow persisted. "Mr. Cunningham, I need to know in order to improve."

It was one time too many. "John," Cunningham had answered, "I just don't care."

"But Mr. Cunningham," Biglow began, "don't you want me to improve . . ."

"John," said Cunningham, "your mother wants to see you improve. Your father wants to see you improve. But me, I just don't give a good goddamn . . ."

But Cunningham was also aware that John Biglow might become an outstanding oarsman. He was eminently teachable, and he had the one critical quality required of any serious oarsman. He was, in Cunningham's phrase, "an obsessive-compulsive," and all good oarsmen had to commit more to this sport than it was actually worth. In addition, John Biglow had high athletic intelligence, a sense of the sport and a certain daring. In a race during his junior year, the crew had gone out very high and after several hundred yards were down a length. At that point Biglow had brought the stroke down four notches. It was an unusual move, something that almost no other seventeen-year-old would have been willing to risk. The response of almost every other stroke would have been to send the stroke higher, or go for power tens. Instead, Biglow had steadied his boat, allowed it to find its tempo, and the Lakeside boat had come together, catching even and then surging ahead. He had been ecstatic after the race. "Mr. Cunningham, Mr. Cunningham," he had shouted, "it worked! It worked!"

Cunningham had no idea how far Biglow would go, but there were signs the next year, when Biglow stroked the varsity. He was more serious about rowing than some of the others and determined that high standards of seriousness should prevail. He was angry when the others did not concentrate or care as much as he did. One day when there was too much talking behind him, he told one of the oarsmen that if he talked about anything other than rowing, he, John Biglow, was going to throw the offender in the water. When the warning was not heeded and the boat came back to the boathouse, Biglow did indeed throw the oarsman in the water and then, just for good measure, jumped in himself, perhaps to show that going in the water was not so bad a fate and perhaps to prevent anyone else from throwing him in.

His relationship with Cunningham remained one of mutual admiration mixed with mutual grievance. Part of the reason may have been that John, because of the tensions with his father, always wanted his coaches to play a larger role in his life than they really could. In subtle ways he expressed his belief that Cunningham both demanded too much and did not push the crew enough or place enough emphasis on winning. On Cunningham's side, there was a belief, also expressed in subtle ways, that John had not yet grown up and used his unusual sensitivity to manipulate people to get what he wanted. It appeared that he would go to Yale, which had shown interest in him. Compared to recruiting for sports such as football and basketball, Yale's courtship was mild, a few phone calls from a freshman coach and a few letters. But it was recruiting nonetheless.

That summer he worked out in a pair with a Lakeside friend named Paul Most. Biglow's mother later referred to it as the summer he rowed, ate, slept and went out rowing again. Their training was serious. After shopping around for advice, they gradually put together a schedule. For the first time Biglow pushed himself to reach for extra power, to punish himself at a level far greater than in the past. He and Most decided they wanted to enter some kind of regatta, but all the regattas were back East. Finally they selected the national championships, which were in Philadelphia that summer. Their headmaster knew the Penn crew coach, Ted Nash, and he arranged for them to use a boat. They entered the intermediate category, which, Biglow later learned, was a mistake. They were good enough to enter the elite. They rowed very well and came in second. Biglow was surprised at how easy it had been, and he was annoyed after the race that Most, his bowman, had not told him there was one boat still ahead of them. They might have won the whole thing. For the first time, Biglow sensed what he might be able to do in rowing.

Yale was supposed to be inevitable for a Biglow. His brother Lucius had applied and received an unlikely, which meant that there was only a 1 percent chance that he would be admitted. But his father had pulled strings, and Lucius had been let in. Yale had not been a pleasant experience for him. The bright people seemed too bright, and the athletes were better than he was; later he transferred to Boston University. John, therefore, had been wary of following the family footsteps to Yale. He applied there dutifully, but he intended to go to Williams. But he failed to get into Williams, and the only two schools that accepted him were the University of Washington and Yale. He did not want to stay at home; Yale, therefore, it would be.

When he entered Yale, he was torn between going out for soccer and rowing. He was unsure of himself academically and socially, and he knew that he wanted to be part of something that gave him a sense of self and a sense of belonging. When he turned to his brother for advice, Luke Biglow asked him what he wanted out of athletics. John Biglow's answer was odd for someone contemplating rowing: He wanted fun.

"In that case," said Luke, "you probably ought to try rowing—they seem to have a lot of camaraderie."

John rowed on the first Yale freshman crew to beat Harvard in thirteen years, but even then he was not sure he was ready to make a full commitment. He was also in a singing group, and he liked singing and had a good voice. In the end he decided his rowing friendships were more important than his singing friendships. Because the oarsmen all had to sacrifice so much for the sport, their relationships with each other were far more intense.

The commitment to rowing, once made, was complete. He held back nothing. The Yale program had been in disarray since the early 1960s. When John Biglow entered Yale in the fall of 1976, Harvard had won the annual four-mile race every year since 1963 and had dominated almost all of eastern rowing as well. Yale rowing had become a backwater, and an aura of defeat hung about the boathouse. In the early 1970s, the Yale coaches had a hard time even putting together a second heavyweight freshman crew. In rowing, it was traditional for the losers to give their rowing shirts to the winners. The customary Yale rowing shirt was fancy and by no means inexpensive, blue with white trim and a satin sash. So many of these shirts had been given away that by the 1970s the school had started sending its young men out in simple blue T-shirts. But in 1975, the nucleus of some very good Yale crews began to assemble.

The next year Steve Kiesling, Dave Potter and Eric Stephens, as well as Biglow, were added. From the start there was no doubt that Biglow's was an exceptional presence. But he was often difficult, even for those who liked him. He insisted on calling Tony Johnson "Mister Tony," as if he were a little boy at summer camp talking to the head counselor. ("What are we going to do today, Mr. Tony?" he would ask, and Johnson would that they were going to do 3-minute pieces. "Will it be hard on us, Mr. Tony?" he would ask. Johnson would answer that yes, indeed, it might very well be hard. "Will it be hard on you, Mr. Tony?" he would ask.

Johnson said that no, he was going to coach so it would not be very hard on him.)

Johnson handled Biglow with great skill. He did not challenge Biglow, and he did not make his games seem more serious than they were. Johnson realized he had a superb and dedicated athlete who was reflecting ambivalence about who and where he was by playing games. But on important things—training, discipline, concentration—no corners were cut. Biglow never cheated. If anything, he was an enforcer who helped the coach. Biglow himself was not only a great oar but he also pushed others, by his skills and by the fact that such extraordinary ergometer scores came from so modest a body, to be better. Mildly irritating and abrasive he might be, but no one doubted his seriousness as an athlete or his desire to compete. Whether he chose to grow up in other areas was his own business.

Johnson did not force confrontation, and he accepted Biglow at face value. If Biglow came down to the boathouse before breakfast and asked too many questions, Johnson usually did not cut him off. But one day Biglow asked too many questions, and Johnson turned to him and said, "John, we have thirty people on this squad. If I answer a lot of questions from all of them, I won't have time for anything else. So you can ask only one question." Biglow asked his question, looking very much like a little boy. Afterward, there was a long silence. Then Biglow, his face a little sheepish, asked, "Mister Tony, do you think it's all right if I ask one for Dave Potter, too?" On another occasion, during a long and exhausting early-spring workout in Florida, John Biglow looked up from his oar, pointed to a bird and asked, "What kind of bird is that, Mr. Tony?" The next day Tony Johnson had a bird watcher's guide with him in the launch and dutifully tried to figure out which bird was which. Later, as they all walked past the University of Tampa library, Johnson noticed a large number of unusual birds. "Do you know what those are, John?" he asked. "No," Biglow said. "John," said Johnson, who had been studying the guidebook the night before, "those are yellow-crowned night herons." He took the guidebook and handed it to Biglow. He was terribly pleased with himself.

Johnson, coaching in the shadow of Harry Parker, his job jeopardized because of the Yale losing streak, knew that he had finally come across some exceptional oarsmen. He was a distinguished oarsman himself, holding a silver medal from the 1968 Olympics in the pair without cox (he and his partner had lost in the last ten yards to the East Germans by about four feet or, by the clock, 7:26.56 to 7:26.71). He was not nearly as intense as Parker. If by the standards of mere mortals Johnson seemed obsessive, in the world of rowing his relative normality was regarded as being the sign of an eccentric. In the beginning he had not pushed his Yale crews that hard. He was learning about coaching just as they were learning about rowing. There was if not a country-club atmosphere to Yale rowing when he arrived, certainly a great deal less than total commitment. Andy Fisher, coxswain of some of the Johnson crews, had been appalled in his sophomore year to go to a March team meeting where the senior Yale oarsmen had talked of their goals for the coming season. Goals for the coming season? It was March, and it was too late to talk about goals. The season was about to start, and Harry Parker's crews had been in rigorous training since September. The new rowers joining the Yale program had that intensity, the old ones did not and the Yale boathouse was divided. Some of the more senior oarsmen looked down on people such as Bouscaren and Fisher because they were too brash, and on Biglow because he was not hip; in turn, the three younger men barely managed to veil their contempt for those who did not care enough.

To John Biglow, the great thing that Tony Johnson taught his athletes was that there were no limits to what they could force their bodies to do. Johnson would say this again and again. The limits were only in the mind, not in the body. In the struggle between the mind and the body, the mind would win if the body had been pushed hard during practice. Thus Johnson pushed them to work harder and harder on the weight machines, to do one more repetition; and they would do it, almost screaming with pain, their friends helping them to move their legs on the machines when they could no longer continue without help. The body in effect had given up, and it was being manipulated by the mind. That was what Johnson meant by expanding the limits.

Bouscaren always wanted to analyze what they were doing and why. He was not just an athlete but also a student of sports, and occasionally his questions got under Johnson's skin. One day when the oarsmen were doing weight repetitions, Bouscaren suggested they might try more repetitions of lighter weights. Johnson, normally mild and careful, simply said, "Shut up and do it." What he was saying, in effect, was "Joe, you think too much, and it hurts your rowing." (In 1984, with both Bouscaren and Biglow preparing for the Olympics, Bouscaren had gone to see Yale race at a regatta in Cambridge. "Did you see Tony?" Biglow asked him. "Yes," said Bouscaren. "What did he say?" Biglow asked. " 'Don't think too much,' " Bouscaren replied.)

No one in those four years pushed himself as hard as John Biglow. On occasion the others found it hard to live up to his standards. His concentration was so exceptional that he could tell if someone in the boat was not putting out. When that happened, he would become furious. The pain of rowing was as hard on him as on others, but he tried to hide it as much as he could. From time to time he would tell Fisher, the cox (no one else but the cox), "I just don't want to do it today. It hurts too much." Fisher would nod, and Biglow would keep rowing harder than anyone else in the boat. Years later, as a champion single sculler, he did his Nautilus workouts just before going out for his sculling workouts. There was a reason for this. In the Nautilus workouts, it was easy to calibrate pain. If, after a certain number of repetitions, he hit terrible pain, he could, by doing a few more repetitions, tell how final the pain was and whether he could push through it or not. Then, when he went out on the water and encountered the same level of pain, he could calibrate how much more he could push because he had just done the same thing on the machines.

Biglow's freshman crew had almost won the Eastern Sprints. In his sophomore year he rowed the number-two oar, and the Yale varsity began to win. In the same season, 1978, Yale went back to its fancier rowing shirts. That June Fisher told Johnson that he thought Biglow was too great a talent to be rowing the number-two oar; he should stroke the boat, he was so natural a leader. Johnson had been thinking much the same thing, and in his junior year John Biglow stroked the 1979 Yale boat, one of the great crews in Yale history.

His relationship with his teammates was always complex. In his junior year, the seniors, some of whom represented the old guard of Yale rowing, named him Ball and Mallet. It was a traditional Yale rowing position but not one many many people aspired to, for the Ball and Mallet was, in truth, a bit of a buffoon. It was his job to organize the bus trips and make sure there were cookies on them and take care of the croquet games played at Gales Ferry while waiting for the Harvard race. Frequently the B and M came from the jayvee or the third boat. The Ball and Mallet never lost at the croquet games because he could make up the rules as the games went along, which was one of the few benefits of the job. It was a job that diminished the holder; and in the case of Biglow, that aim was, his friends thought, quite deliberate. The designation had come as something of a surprise to Biglow, and he was not pleased. It was the old guard's way of saying, "All right, you may be a great oar, but we are going to remind you that you remain an outsider."

The B and M was known as the Boy. "Boy," the others would call, "Boy, we want some cookies." At the first meeting, Biglow had tried to set his rules as the Boy. The Boy, he had said, would be fair. The Boy would be just. The Boy would try to earn the respect of everyone there. And the Boy would be Nuts as a Bunny. But he did not do a very good job as the Boy, and it was, when all the jokes were done, demeaning.

In John Biglow's junior year, the Yale crew was favored over Harvard for probably the first time in almost 20 years. Yale had already won the Eastern Sprints, beating Harvard among others, and its only loss had been against a relatively weak Dartmouth crew in water so rough that the Yale boat nearly sank. This was an exceptionally big crew, six-four and 200 pounds on the average, bigger than Harvard and almost, it seemed, cocky.

Even within the punishing world of rowing, the Harvard-Yale race stands apart. Most races are two thousand meters or roughly a mile and a quarter. The Harvard-Yale race, rowed every year on the Thames in New London, is four miles. It is the equivalent of a football team that plays all its games in sixty minutes, going for one final championship game lasting three hours. It is a unique test of stamina and courage. In 1978, Dave Potter, the Yale stroke, had been suffering from a bad back and he had virtually passed out after three miles despite the attempts of Andy Fisher to splash water on his face. The Yale boat had lagged accordingly, and Harvard had won by two lengths. That was considered a great race, but the 1979 race stands apart.

"I doubt that there was ever a better one before," said Harry Parker, "and I doubt that there will be a better one again." Because Yale had started too tentatively in 1978, Biglow was determined to bring his crew out very quickly. That he did, bringing Yale out very high, a thirty-eight for the beginning and then settling at a thirty-six for the rest of the race. It was a punishing beat, but it seemed to work. At two miles Yale held a length lead, which was in one sense a great deal and in another very little, given how furious the Yale pace had been and potentially how much it might have taken out of the oarsmen. At 2½ miles, Harvard pulled even. If Biglow was stroking brilliantly for Yale, then Gordie Gardiner was stroking just as brilliantly for Harvard. Steve Kiesling, rowing behind Biglow, watching the two of them out of the corner of his eye, had a feeling that there were two races, one between Harvard and Yale and a separate and private one between Biglow and Gardiner. For a time the lead went back and forth, depending on whose oars had last been in the water—first Harvard, then Yale, then Harvard, then Yale. Each crew was trying to row through its opponent, but neither crew would break. With about a mile left, Harvard went ahead by a length. That, thought Harry Parker, is probably the race. Usually, in a case when crews that have battled evenly for that long and that hard and then one rows through the other, the feat represents a triumph of will that is geometrically amplified. The crew that surges feels stronger and more confident, and that strength and confidence generate more power; the one that has been passed feels weaker, and the mind releases the body from its earlier resolve. But at the very end, Biglow brought the Yale crew back, and it once again began gaining on Harvard. There was too little time left, and one Yale oarsman missed a stroke, and Harvard won. Four seconds over four miles.

The members of the Yale crew that day still see that race and still feel each stroke. They remember with remarkable clarity each surge by both boats; and when they talk about their college rowing, the talk will inevitably come back to that race. They still seek an answer to what went wrong. Some of them think, Biglow may have taken Yale out too high. But they were a powerful crew, and they had been ready. Just as possibly, if Biglow had taken them out lower, Harvard might have surged ahead earlier. Perhaps that Crimson crew was simply too good. Earlier in the year, when Harvard had won in a race at San Diego, one of the Harvard oarsmen had stood up and yelled to his teammates, "Oh, you Harvard gods!" In the 1979 race, Andy Fisher mocked that. Each time Yale pulled ahead, instead of saying, "I have one seat . . . I have two seats on Harvard," he said to his crew, "I have one Harvard god . . . I have two Harvard gods . . ." It is at once their most cherished memory and their most troubling one. They had rowed so well, they were such a good crew and they had lost.

The next year Biglow did not stroke but rowed the six oar instead. There was a feeling that he might be too good an oar to stroke the boat, that his pace was too demanding for the others to keep up with. But Yale did not win the following year, either. It simply unraveled in the last mile, and that was almost as bitter. The careers of the Yale crew were finished, oddly incomplete. Even though they had been part of the renaissance of Yale rowing, even though they had been a great crew and rowed magnificently, they had never beaten Harvard.

John Biglow left college uncertain of his future. He had, like most of his teammates, devoted himself so fully to rowing, had been so completely encapsulated in that world, that he did not know what he wanted to do with the rest of his life. The oarsmen had committed themselves to something at an almost professional level, but unlike other sports, rowing offered no professional career to follow through with. At twenty-one and twenty-two the crew's pseudoprofessional incarnations were over, and they had to start their lives again.

Biglow seemed particularly lost. He thought of medical school, but he had not done particularly well as an undergraduate, and he had not been premed. He had broken up with his girlfriend; even worse, she had gone off with another Yale oarsman. The parting had been bitter and acrimonious, and air had mysteriously disappeared from the other oarsman's tires. A little lost, his life vague now without the single-minded focus of rowing, John Biglow returned to Seattle to live at home and ponder his future. Because there was an immense vacuum in his life and because he did not know what to do with himself, he started working out in a single scull.

Back in Seattle he sought coaching from both Cunningham and McIntyre, even though the relationship with

Cunningham remained an uneven one. To the early uneasiness was added Cunningham's dislike of Biglow's emphasis on strength and endurance at the cost of technique. For a long time those tensions did not flare up, and their mutual love for rowing kept them friendly. Then, in the winter of 1983, they had a major confrontation. The origin of their confrontation was somewhat ironic. In 1983 John Biglow had suggested to Harry Parker, the coach of the national team, that it might be a good idea to have Frank Cunningham accompany the national team to the world championships as a boat repairman, a field in which he was an expert hand. Cunningham had retired some 3 years earlier after 30 years of teaching in Seattle, and he was then doing free-lance coaching and repairing boats.

Biglow, annoyed by Cunningham and McIntyre's criticism of his style, made the suggestion of the European trip in the hope of proving to Cunningham that a boat could move well without expert technique and that a boat with exceptional technique often moved slowly. Harry Parker, who did not know Biglow's reason, had been slightly puzzled but, knowing Cunningham's skills, he had quickly assented. But if John Biglow intended to teach Frank Cunningham a lesson, he picked the wrong trip. The American team had not done well. The most successful oarsman had been Tiff Wood, who had gotten a bronze in the single. In Cunningham's view, even Tiff had won in spite of himself, and Cunningham had been appalled by the wasted effort in the young man's style. Biglow had stroked the quad, which came in seventh. Cunningham had not kept his feelings about the poor showing entirely secret, but there had been no confrontation between Cunningham and Biglow. That came later that year when Bruce Beall, one of the Harvard coaches, was in Seattle.

There had been a dinner party at the Biglows' house, and Cunningham had been invited for a collegial evening of rowing men at which Lucius Biglow's home movies of the world championships would be shown. But before dinner, while everyone was sitting around talking, someone had passed around pictures of the races. One of them showed the American eight rowing with an almost total lack of symmetry in a sport that depended upon its precision. The picture was passed to Cunningham. "Grotesque," he said and laughed. The moment he made the remark he knew it was a mistake, and he regretted it. John Biglow, enraged, his face taut with anger, had got up and made a formal speech. Later he realized he wanted to hurt Cunningham. "You and my father may talk about these photos after the race movies are shown. But not before. I do not want to hear anything more from you right now."

In time the race movies were shown, and in Cunningham's opinion they *were* grotesque. Afterward Biglow had sought Cunningham out. Cunningham, he said, had no right to be so critical of the national team. It was clear that Cunningham, having made the trip at Biglow's suggestion, had in some way betrayed him by being critical in Biglow's own house. Cunningham had thought, Well, this is all right, this is John defending his teammates who in his eyes worked so hard for that race. That was understandable. It was also, he suspected, John finally showing that he, too, was an adult and no longer a boy. Why else had he included his father in his denunciation of Cunningham? Well, that, too, was acceptable. Then it became personal. Biglow told Cunningham that his expectations of others had always been too high, that he had been too impatient and not sympathetic enough to young oarsmen. We are, Cunningham thought, talking about something a little different now. He had not tried to rebut Biglow, but he had left the house upset and feeling that in some way he had been dressed down by a young prince. For several weeks Cunningham heard nothing from John Biglow and assumed the relationship was finished. But then, about two months later, Biglow and his friend Paul Enquist showed up wondering if Cunningham could help them work on the double for the upcoming Olympics. No mention was made of the dinner party.

CHAPTER
SEVENTEEN

If rowing was an estimable sport filled with virtue and honor and strength, then there was something about the team camps that was the reverse of that. They became its Darwinian lowest common denominator. This camp was, if anything, worse; it was filled with anxiety and tension that turned inevitably into paranoia. So much depended on so little that was quantifiable. From the fourteen oarsmen invited, Parker had merely five weeks to pick both the double and the quad. In most sports the selection would be easy: Simply keep the various oarsmen racing against each other in singles and pick the top six. But crew was different; the whole was not the sum of its parts. A quad filled with four scullers of medium power who had perfected their technique might easily beat one filled with the camp's four most powerful scullers. Nor did making a camp boat necessarily mean that an oarsman would go to the Olympics. There was to be an additional Olympic trial at Princeton in June at which other boats, some of them filled with men who chose not to go to the camp, some filled with young men scorned by Parker (their motivation thus all the higher), had the right to challenge the camp boats. Since these boats, doubles and quads, were already practicing together and since the camp-boat crews might not be picked for several weeks, the outsiders had a certain advantage in rowing together, if not in natural gifts. The possibility of one of them winning the trials added to the element of paranoia at the camp.

Every sculler in those tense moments was watching Harry Parker, wondering if he was on Parker's good or bad side and wondering what Parker, so quiet and enigmatic, really thought. In this hothouse atmosphere old friends first became rivals and then enemies, while old rivals in the new juxtaposition of loyalties became allies. In addition, some of the oarsmen, Jim Dietz among them, did not like Harry Parker and knew that he did not like them. If most of the oarsmen called him "Harry" and spoke of him as a kind of rowing deity, Dietz referred to him as "Parker" and thought of him as an enemy. Those who had studied Harry Parker closely knew that his selections were an odd mixture of rationality and scientology. He was the master of seat racing, which both in Harvard practices and in his camps he had brought to its most savage form; but he also trusted his own instincts, and he valued other rowing skills that did not show in seat racing but that won races. In camps he sometimes protected certain oarsmen whose skills he was confident of from the savagery of the seat racing by keeping exposure to a minimum or by creating an environment in which they would not lose. He would use stronger oarsmen as cannon fodder to wear out the oarsmen he did not really want. Would Harry play favorites with Tiff and Joe and Charley because they had rowed for him in Cambridge? If Harry was letting Tiff row with Charley Altekruse, did that mean that he had already decided on them for the double?

Tiff Wood never doubted that he would make the double or the quad. Nor was he in any way wary of Harry Parker. If there was one person in Wood's life over the past thirteen years who symbolized what he wanted to be, it was Harry Parker.

The camp did not begin well for Tiff. His disappointment over losing in Princeton was evident, and it soon became clear to him that his sole objective there had been winning the single sculls. For a time he thought of leaving the camp and competing in the singles at the international regatta at Lake Lucerne. The idea was not really a serious one, but it showed how important being a single sculler had been to him. His life for three years had been built around one goal, and now he had fallen short of that goal. Going back to rowing in team boats was harder than he had expected. He had spent the past four years rowing by himself, and he had been his own master. If he rowed roughly, he had also rowed strongly, and he had disturbed no one else's timing. He had difficulty adjusting now that he was back in team boats; it was as if the better he had gotten in the single, the worse he had gotten in team boats.

The camp was a game of musical chairs in which there were bound to be a lot of losers. Besides, those who knew Parker found him unusually distracted this year. Part of the problem was that even as he was coaching the single scullers in Hanover he was preparing a rather ordinary Harvard crew for its four-mile race against Yale. After Harvard's long ascendancy over Yale, Yale had won the past three races; and other crews, not just Yale, were catching up to him. Coaches elsewhere were now imitating his year-round training methods; and some were recruiting more actively than he, for it was the part of the job he liked least and was least suited for. He did not like going to a young man and encouraging him to come to a college where he might not even make the program.

In addition, he was fighting his own personal disappointment. He was accustomed to being the preeminent figure of American rowing, and he had wanted to be the coach of both the sweeps and the scullers. Originally, the Olympic committee had set up specifications for the sweep job that would permit the coach to divide his time between his college team and the Olympic crew. Harry Parker had, accordingly, made his proposal to the Olympic committee. But even as he was doing this, the Olympic committee, bothered by the generally poor performance of American oarsmen in recent Olympiads, changed its mind, in part because Kris Korzeniowski, a talented Polish coach in exile from his homeland, was available. Korzeniowski was willing to serve as a full-time national coach who would spend an entire year working with the national talent available without any other responsibilities. Suddenly the job specifications changed dramatically. The Olympic rowing committee chose Korzeniowski to coach the sweeps and left Parker only the scullers. The fact that the Olympic rowing committee had picked a foreigner, scorning the best of the American coaches, had devastated Parker. After years of being unchallenged, he felt betrayed and he protested the committee's decision in the most personal terms. In his mind the committee was giving his rowers to another coach, and he never entirely reconciled himself to his diminished status.

On the day of the Princeton trials there had been a brief flare-up between Parker and Charley Altekruse. Altekruse had not qualified for the final; but he was supposed to row in what was called the *petit* final, a consolation event that would give the standing for the next six oarsmen, places eight through thirteen. *Petit* finals were normally not important; but for a sculling coach trying to make selections for an Olympic camp, they had a relatively high priority. Altekruse's decision to skip the *petit* final had angered Parker. Even though Altekruse was one of his favorite oarsmen, Parker had taken Altekruse aside and had told him that he did not like his attitude. To his surprise, Altekruse had then told him that he didn't like *Parker's* attitude, that he did not seem committed to the Olympic sculling team and that the scullers felt that they were being neglected because of his disappointment about not coaching the sweep oarsmen.

Altekruse's response had surprised Parker, and a few days later, Parker called Tiff Wood to tell him what had happened. Wood felt that during their talk Parker had, in fact, confirmed that Altekruse was essentially right—he *had* been disappointed in not getting the eight, and it *had* affected him. When Harvard oarsmen of the past heard what Altekruse had said, they were staggered; no one would have dared talk to Harry like that fifteen years earlier.

In Hanover Parker quickly decided that all the concentration on the single-sculls final had set the team back considerably. As a coach, Parker had been as fair as he could to Wood, Biglow and Bouscaren but had privately hoped for Wood's victory in the singles. The difference between Wood and Biglow was negligible—if one could win a bronze, the other surely could. But Biglow was a considerable asset in the team boats, and Wood more limited there. It soon became clear that Tiff Wood was not going to have an easy time in the camp.

Parker was quiet and distant in the early weeks of the seat racing; and the quieter he was, the greater the tension became. There was no doubt that he favored Charley Altekruse and Joe Bouscaren in the double. Wood was at first annoyed, then worried. The more anxious he became, the more he sought to push through solely on power, and the rougher he rowed. He was not sure that anyone was having that good a camp. As far as he was concerned, only Altekruse was doing well. Altekruse had not rowed strongly in the Princeton single trials, but he seemed to be cresting here. He was a powerful oarsman, still in transition from sweep oarsman to sculler. On the basis of his pure aerobic ability, he was viewed by his peers as the equal of Biglow and Wood. Wood could understand Parker's thinking: Altekruse, a great racer, as strong or stronger than anyone in the camp; and Bouscaren, a formidable sculler of exceptional skill.

But Wood thought Parker's decision misguided. In a major regatta, where there would be a series of races, endurance became a factor and he was stronger than Bouscaren. In addition, because Bouscaren was so mechanically skilled as an oarsman, his boat was likely to be as good on the first day of practice as it was several weeks later. Another double, perhaps one that paired him, Wood, with Altekruse or Lewis or Biglow, might not be so efficient in the beginning, but it would have more power to harness. Long after the Al-tekruse-Bouscaren boat hit its plateau and stopped improving, the other boat was likely to become stronger. Wood wanted Parker to *project* the idea of power in a boat, not just seize on what was immediately happening at the camp. Wood also thought that he was being paired with lesser oarsmen too often and not being given enough chances to row with some of the other top scullers, such as Jim Dietz, Paul Enquist and Brad Lewis. Wood soon believed that his only chance lay in the quad, and the quad was being stroked by a young man named Charley Bracken, whose stroke he had a difficult time following.

Brad Lewis shared Tiff Wood's sense of frustration. Lewis had come to camp in a relatively good mood. He knew there had been unspoken tensions between him and Harry Parker in the past. (A few years earlier, coming East with his shell, he had asked Tiff Wood to ask Harry for a storage rack in the Harvard boathouse; it was better, he had said, if Tiff inquired, since he and Harry did not get along that well.) But in that sculling camp summer of 1983, Harry Parker had placed Lewis in a good double, and he and Paul Enquist had finished a respectable sixth in the world. The Hanover camp seemed fair but puzzling to Lewis. He rowed with Altekruse and Bouscaren. The one person he wanted to row with and did not was Tiff Wood. At one point Lewis went up to Chris Allsopp, Parker's assistant, and asked to be paired with Tiff. For Lewis that was the most natural pairing, since he and Wood had finished two, three in the single trial. If the combination worked, it would be a very good boat. Allsopp said he would think about it, but nothing ever happened.

Lewis did not like Hanover. It rained every day, and the rooms were small and damp and had no phones. His cousin Mitch had accompanied him, and there were some complaints about Mitch's clothes. Since Mitch went through life wearing sweat suits and Brad did not want his cousin to feel out of place, he spent $20 on some eastern clothes for him.

Like Wood, Brad had concentrated so much on the single

that the return to team boats was difficult. He did not do as well in seat racing as he should have. Although he thought Altekruse and Bouscaren's success in the seat racing legitimate, he was not so sure they were that good a double. That boat seemed to him a particular kind of coach's choice, what he called a "click combination." If a coach put two oarsmen together and they immediately clicked, becoming a fast boat from the start, the coach was happy.

Even so, his best chance, like Wood's, was in the double, not the quad. The double was an easier boat for oarsmen who were strong instead of graceful, and it was easier to put together at the last minute. The quad, which placed a premium on combined experience and smoothness of group technique, was a difficult boat for Americans. It often went at very high strokes, deftly rather than powerfully executed. The best quad in the world probably was the West German one, and there the same four oarsmen had been rowing together since 1977. The quad at this camp was likely to be stroked by Charley Bracken, and Lewis also had trouble rowing behind Bracken. Since he had no memory of ever seeing Bracken before, he asked one of the other oarsmen if Bracken had rowed at the Princeton trials. His friend said he had. "How did he do?" Lewis asked. "He didn't make the semifinals," the friend answered.

With Bracken stroking Lewis's boat, Brad felt as if he were riding a bicycle backward. He did not think it was Bracken's fault any more than it was his own. In one race their quad had lost by six lengths. Lewis had never been beaten like that in his life. Then he and Bill Purdy switched seats. This time the boat Lewis had just left beat the one he had just joined. He could not remember a worse day on the water.

CHAPTER
EIGHTEEN

On the eve of the Lake Lucerne trip, Parker made his cuts. Even before he was cut, Jim Dietz, who knew the ax was coming, and Parker exchanged harsh words. Dietz did not hesitate to express his feeling that he had never been given a fair chance. The boats had seemed virtually set from the beginning. The double, to no one's surprise, was Altekruse and Bouscaren. *The Love Boat*, Lewis had nicknamed it, because Altekruse and Bouscaren were both good-looking and both aware of the effect of their good looks upon young women. Three of the oars in the quad were Sean Colgan, Bill Purdy and Charley Bracken. Wood and a younger sculler named Jack Frackleton would fight it out on Lucerne for the fourth spot. Parker asked Brad Lewis if he would come as the eighth man. Lewis was not enthusiastic; to him that was the position of a spare, and the real spare would be the loser of the Wood-Frackleton struggle. Lewis called the job being offered to him "the fair spare," just someone to hold hands with the other oarsmen. He was very unhappy. He did not want to be in so subordinate a position, hoping that something happened to one of the other oarsmen so he could get a chance and all the while believing in his heart that he was better than anyone in the quad. He told Allsopp that he was thinking of quitting the program. Allsopp reported his words to

Parker, and Parker said that that was all right but he wanted an answer by 5:00 P.M. that day.

That afternoon Lewis drove to Boston with Bouscaren and his girlfriend. The trip took three hours, and on the way Lewis got out a pad and listed all the pros and cons of Parker's offer. The pros were that it was a chance to compete at Lucerne, which was the major regatta of the year; and there was a possibility that if either boat did poorly in Switzerland, he would get another chance. He would get a chance to row with Tiff in a double, albeit with very little time to practice together. The cons were powerful, however. He had no real role. His position would be subservient, and he rowed in the first place so he would not have to be subservient. Besides rowing with Tiff in the double, Lewis would also have to row with Frackleton and was convinced that would be a slow boat. The circumstances would not bring out his best. His mistake at the camp had been his failure to insist that he row the double with Tiff. They should have forced the issue, having earned the right by rowing two, three in the singles final.

On the way into Boston he and Bouscaren and Bouscaren's girlfriend had sat for a long time in stalled traffic in the steaming heat on one of the Boston–Cambridge bridges. As they came off, there had been a question of which way they turned to get to the Harvard boathouse. Did they follow a sign that said "Back Bay" or one that said "Somerville–Cambridge"? Lewis had said "Back Bay," the girlfriend said "Somerville–Cambridge" and Bouscaren had not known. Lewis was sure that the girlfriend was mistaken, and Bouscaren had listened to her and turned the wrong way. Lewis looked at Bouscaren a long time. He's taking instructions from a *girl* and a girl who doesn't know what the hell she's talking about, Lewis thought. His rules of masculine-feminine behavior were seriously offended. With that he decided that Bouscaren was weak and he could beat him and so right then he decided not to go to Lucerne. He only hoped that Harry would not change the boatings.

Lewis went to the Harvard boathouse and found Paul Enquist. He asked Enquist if he wanted to challenge the camp boat of Altekruse and Bouscaren. Enquist said he did. Just to be sure that he was not too close to the situation and acting on emotion, Lewis called his father in California. "Quit," his father said, "they aren't giving you enough respect." So Brad Lewis phoned Harry Parker.

"I'm going to come to Lucerne," he began.

"That's good," Parker said.

"But only if Paul and I can row in a second double," he added. "We'll pay our own way. All expenses. All we want is to be allowed to enter as the other double."

Parker thought for a moment. "I don't think that's a very practical idea," he said. In that case, Lewis told him, he would row with Enquist as a challenge boat.

Parker then phoned back to the boathouse and offered the position of the spare to Enquist, who turned it down. That's silly of Harry to call me when Brad's just told him I'm his partner, Enquist thought. The phone call angered Lewis because Parker was trying to break up his team. Parker, of course, was furious because he thought Lewis was breaking up *his* team.

Lewis and Enquist then took a double that belonged to the Olympic committee off the trailer that was returning it from Hanover to the Harvard boathouse. They put the double on a van and drove off to Lake Squam to start their workouts. It was not clear whether they had a right to the boat. Possession seemed to be nine tenths of the law. While they were doing that, Harry Parker was calling other men he had just cut, trying to get one of them to become the spare. Ridgley Johnson first accepted the offer and then turned it down, deciding to row in a challenging quad. Then Parker called Greg Montessi, who also turned him down. Only seven oarsmen went to Europe, not eight as originally planned. Old Harvard oarsmen had never seen Harry Parker so livid.

In Europe the scullers did not do particularly well. John

Biglow had gone ahead to Granau, East Germany, where he had rowed badly and did not even make the finals. His confidence was clearly shaken despite the fact that he had not sent a boat ahead and was rowing in a tub. At Lucerne he had done better but not as well as he or Parker had wanted. He was not peaking as the Olympics neared. The double took fourth and fifth—good, not great; the quad rowed back-to-back races for two days. With Tiff Wood rowing it came in fourth, with Jack Frackleton rowing the next day it came in third. Wood was now the underdog in the fight for the last place in the quad; and because Parker had a limited period to get the quad ready and was now giving the major share of time in the boat to Frackleton, Wood's chances were further diminished. The team flew back to America from Switzerland, took one day off, drove to the camp in Hanover and rowed lightly on the evening of Tuesday, the nineteenth. Harry, it was rumored, would announce the final boatings on the following Monday.

CHAPTER
NINETEEN

Tiff Wood's fall from grace in so short a time was terrible and almost complete. Six weeks earlier he had been the defending world bronze medal holder and the reigning American champion. Now it appeared that he would not make a boat at all. At the trials in Princeton, his time in the semifinals had been some 29 seconds better than Frackleton's, a staggering differential. But the word from the others in the quad was that the boat seemed heavier with Wood in it. He was trying desperately to keep control of himself and not come apart. He was absolutely sure that he was better than Frackleton and some of the others, that with real seat racing, which had always saved him in the past, he could win. He simply would not accept the idea that he could not row in a team boat. In the late 1970s, before he had moved to the single, he and Gregg Stone had rowed in a very fast double that had taken second at Henley in 1977 ; and a year later, with Chris Allsopp, the assistant coach at this camp, he had taken fifth in the world. Then in 1979, preparing for the Olympics, Wood and many of the other scullers had put their efforts into team boats, not the singles. He had been part of a very good quad that Al Shealy had stroked, and they had become better and better. They had intended to row the quad in the Olympics and had been confident that they could surprise the Europeans, but the Olympic boycott had torn their world apart.

His present dilemma virtually left him without a means of showing that he was a superior oarsmen. What had always saved him in the past was that he was a great racer, and now he could not save himself by racing. He knew that part of the fault was his own, that he had not rowed well during the camp and that his lapses had taken place under the watch of Harry Parker. If Tiff Wood trusted and believed in anyone in the world of rowing, it was Harry Parker. That faith, however, did not lessen Wood's growing inner rage.

CHAPTER
TWENTY

Brad Lewis and Paul Enquist had gone off almost immediately to practice on Lake Cayuga at Ithaca, New York. If Lewis was a loner, often moody and hard to reach, Enquist was perhaps the easiest man in a rowing camp to get on with. He was always fair, and he never blamed others for his failures. The camp had been a nightmare for him, but he had felt the fault was his. When, at one point, Chris Allsopp had told him that his face lacked intensity while he was rowing, he did not get angry. Instead, he simply wondered why he was not more intense. His ego was not threatened by the loss of a race. Rowing with Paul, thought Bob Ernst, who had coached both men, was as close as Brad could come to being alone in a single. His ego could rule completely. Enquist would never challenge him. When Paul had been cut by Harry from the camp, John Biglow had expected him to be extremely wounded. "Harry was right," Enquist had said, "I wasn't rowing well. I'd have done the same thing."

The son of a commercial salmon fisherman in Seattle, Enquist had gone to Washington State in Pullman; and since he was six-six, he thought he should play basketball. But the coach had not recruited him and therefore seemed to have little interest in a walk-on. When a kindly engineering professor had mentioned crew, which was supposed to be com-

patible for tall people, Enquist had walked down and joined
Washington State's program. The program was new, the
coach was inexperienced and the team always lost. Enquist
rowed in the varsity boat for four years, and in his last year
the crew improved, finishing fourth in the western championships. After graduation in 1977, he worked for a few
months with his father on the salmon boat, but what Paul
really wanted to do was continue rowing. When the salmon
season was finished, he went over to the University of Washington, where Bob Ernst let him work out in a single. Ernst
was coaching the Washington women, and in the morning
he would put a dozen people, most of them women, in singles and let them row. He called them his Mosquito Squad-
ron. Everyone in it was better than Enquist. He did not feel
humiliated by watching smaller women pass him in a scull.
After a year he was as good as most of them. He was big but
he was not strong, and he was only beginning to learn about
training programs. For the next few years he worked at almost nothing but his rowing. His father was underwhelmed.
"Boy, you can't eat those oars," Felix Enquist said.

Each year Paul Enquist worked on his rowing in the winter and then went back East to try himself against the eastern rowers. It took him a long time to make progress. In
1981, he reached the single-scull finals. That summer he took
fourth in the elite finals in the men's national. Still the single
never quite seemed his boat. He was too big, and his cadence
was never right for it. He would get in the single, but no
matter how hard he tried to row at a high pace, he could
never get above twenty-nine. The other oarsmen, amused by
his efforts and by his easygoing disposition, called him Paul
Zenquist. His first breakthrough had come in 1983, after six
years of trying. He had started rowing well in the double and
had made the national team, paired with Brad Lewis. Stoic
and relaxed Enquist might be, Ernst thought, but there was
an enormous drive inside him. It just didn't show in his personality.

In 1983, when Enquist and Lewis had rowed the double, they had not done badly for a young pair—neither of them had very much international experience—but their personal relationship had been extremely difficult. They had taken sixth in the world at Duisburg, limited more by their lack of confidence and experience than by their ability. But when they had returned from Europe to prepare for a regatta at Lake Casitas, Lewis often disappeared on Enquist. Lewis was not at the motel where he was supposed to be staying. He missed practices. He was aloof and distant when he showed. Sometimes, when he did arrive, he was driving a huge white Lincoln. That was not the kind of car an oarsman drove, and it annoyed, if not the accommodating Enquist, some of the other oarsmen. Oarsmen drove Saabs and Volvos. Anyone else might have strangled Brad at that point, but Paul Enquist simply shrugged and said, "Well, Brad *is* different." Partners in a double did not necessarily have to be friends, but they had to accept each other, and this double had seemed to fall below even the acceptable minimal standard.

But now, in 1984 with the Olympics coming up, all of that was past. Lewis thought that Enquist was the almost perfect partner. With his great height and at 215 pounds, he was solid; he learned readily; he made few mistakes and was a powerful finisher. A single was too delicate a boat for him, and he was not good in the quad. The one thing that made Lewis wary was how weak Enquist's forearms were. He was sure that was the reason why Enquist had had problems in close races: His arms had tired at the end. Acting on this belief, Lewis made Enquist start working on weights and was pleased that Enquist was quickly building himself up. Like Lewis, Enquist was highly motivated. They had both come away from the camp frustrated. Lewis had been annoyed by what he felt was the Ivy League cockiness of Altekruse and Bouscaren, the sense they projected that they were in and everyone else was out.

At Ithaca, Tony Johnson, who was coaching the fours both with and without coxswains, was willing to help them. It was the perfect place to train, the water was good and above all there were a lot of boats to race against, for a double with its four oars was well matched against a four, particularly a four with a coxswain. Johnson, a good coach, was in a delicate position. He was helping Lewis and Enquist, but Bouscaren, one of his favorite Yale oarsmen, was in the camp double. Even so, Johnson believed that these were medal-class oarsmen and that they were entitled to some level of help. He got Enquist, who was taller and had an exceptional reach, to shorten up on his stroke so that the angle of his oars was the same as that of Lewis. That alone made the boat go faster. He also thought the pair was rough at the end of the stroke, which was easy to help them with. He had rarely seen such motivated athletes.

At Cornell, Lewis talked every night about their mission. They were hunters out to avenge their wrongs. They would track Altekruse and Bouscaren. Nothing was to break Lewis and Enquist's concentration. Again and again they played a tape from Lewis's California coach, Mike Livingston. It was an unusual tape, set to slightly eerie music that Livingston had composed. "Good day," the tape began, "we are privileged to live another day in this magnificent world. Today you will be tested. Today you will contront your death with the power of your living. As a warrior this is your practice. You must silence your body and senses and quiet your breath and mind that you may create within yourself by act of will the mood of a warrior . . ."

In Ithaca, Lewis and Enquist rowed not only on the water but also in front of mirrors while working on the ergometers. Cut off from the normal world of rowing and coaching, Lewis had always been unusually inventive in creating his own training devices. Once he had invented what he called a speed tube, a piece of rubber tubing he put alongside the boat. If water flowed through it constantly, his speed was high; if it didn't, his boat was lurching. At Newport he had staked out a 250-meter course and had one of his friends, Paula Oberstein, take video movies of his technique. He would work out, come back and check out his form on the video, return and practice his strokes. He would work on his mind by using what he called image rowing. He would sit at the dock in a tank and row a full two-thousand-meter race, setting himself against Tiff Wood and John Biglow, fighting off their challenges. It was important for Lewis to win the image rowing races. At Ithaca, he and Enquist practiced shadow rowing, in which they imagined different racing situations. "One thousand meters," Lewis would say, "and Joe and Charley have just gone out a length." Or: "Five hundred meters to go and I just caught a crab."

He knew they had to expect the unexpected. It was important to be mentally tough, and they could be mentally tough only if they were prepared for any contingency. They had their friends come in and try to distract them while they rowed—concentration was critical. They were going to be the best, he told Enquist. He was sure he had to focus Enquist's mind, make him concentrate more. "No one beats us," he kept saying, "that's our motto—no one beats us." He placed, right in front of the ergometer when they worked every day, a huge chalkboard that said, "No one beats us." Just before the trials he bought a large canvas and a can of spray paint. "No one beats us," he had painted in a ten-foot-long sign.

Then they worked on the water. The key to Lewis was speed. He was sure they had the endurance and the power, for theirs was an unusually big double. But speed was Altekruse and Bouscaren's forte. So every three or four days, he and Enquist did five-hundred-meter sprints to check their time. Steadily it came down. They started at about 1:37. Then 1:34. Then 1:30. Near the end of their stay on Cayuga, they did two five-hundred-meter sprints at 1:29 each, a time not many doubles could match. They were ready. Tony

Johnson, watching them in their last few days, was almost sure they were going to win. He felt a certain twinge of regret about Joe Bouscaren, who would be knocked out of the Olympics, but he hoped that Bouscaren would be made the spare if his double lost.

CHAPTER
TWENTY-ONE

Tiff Wood's friend John Biglow, secure now as the single sculler, watched Wood's pain with immense sympathy. Here was a great rower trapped by forces he could not control. Biglow hated the fact that Wood might miss the Olympics.

"Do you think you've been given a fair chance at this camp?" Biglow asked him.

"No," said Wood, "not at all." His voice did not betray the full rage he felt.

"Well, are you going to talk to Harry about it?" Biglow asked.

"No," Wood said. Biglow asked why not.

"Because I don't think it's an oarsman's job to complain to the coach," he answered.

The tensions in the camp continued to grow. With Frackleton rowing in the quad and Wood virtually without a boat unless he rowed a single, Biglow suggested that he and Wood row a double together. That would allow Biglow to work out without aggravating his back, give Wood a place in a boat and potentially provide some competition for the double. Biglow had made that suggestion earlier, and Parker had been amenable. "We may create some problems for you," Biglow said. "Nothing that I can't deal with," said Parker. Biglow was a passionate oarsman who competed at everything, and for Wood the double was a last desperate chance at an Olympic life. Suddenly the double was intriguing to both of them. Biglow's European tour had not been a success. Based on that trip, not only were Karppinen and Kolbe above him, but even a bronze looked shakier. He had returned home with more doubts about his chances at Casitas than he had left with. But the double was another question. There was no dominating double in the field. If Biglow and Wood combined their talents as world-class rowers well, there was no telling how good they could be. A silver, perhaps even a gold. Altekruse and Bouscaren had taken a fourth and a fifth at Lucerne; if Biglow and Wood could beat them by a couple of seconds, there was a genuine chance for a silver. They tried the double together, and it went well. Parker seemed mildly encouraging. He was aware that he had opened a Pandora's box, that the camp was too tightly charged with someone as strong and admired as Wood not making a boat.

On Wednesday, Parker let the double compete. All the anger and frustration stored up in Wood finally found an outlet. Biglow, his partner, liked to punish himself, anyway. Theirs was not so much a workout as a war. During the competition, which consisted of about fifteen pieces, or segments of twenty strokes each, their faces were astonishing. Everything that was happening in the camp was written on them; they were filled with fury and rage. Wood and Biglow won each piece. Someone mentioned to Parker that the workout had seemed unusually violent. "No worse than Lebanon," he had said.

Afterward Parker was annoyed with the camp double. In the middle of the competition, Altekruse had asked Parker what rate they were supposed to be rowing at. "Charley," Parker had answered, "you're rowing as if this is a race." Bouscaren had fidgeted and complained about the riggings, which Parker interpreted as a sign of anxiety. The double was clearly shaken. Already worried about the Lewis-Enquist challenge, it now had been challenged in the camp.

Parker postponed any further racing on Thursday, no longer so sure that creating a second double had been a good idea. On Friday they raced again, four pieces at a thousand meters. Wood and Biglow won the first by half a length; Altekruse and Bouscaren, the next three by the thinnest of margins. Decisive it might not be, but to Harry Parker it was decisive enough. At that point he called off the idea of a competition between the two doubles. Wood was upset. "But you were the one who encouraged us," he said. "Yes, but I've changed my mind," Parker answered.

Wood, still believing that he was stronger in the double than Bouscaren, asked for a chance to seat-race against him; he would row with Altekruse, and Biglow could row with Bouscaren. Parker seemed surprised by the request. Wood said that he had not had as much time in the boat with Altekruse as he wanted. In fact, he said, he had not had as much time with any of the top racers as he wanted or deserved. But Parker did not want to reopen this question. In his mind the double was set, the quad was a problem and time was very short. "Why didn't you say something to me earlier?" Parker asked. "It's too late now." His reply made Wood so angry he could barely speak. The one thing he hated in rowing camps were oarsmen who lobbied for themselves and coaches who listened to their lobbying. How could Harry miss what had gone on in the camp? How could he miss how Wood felt? Wood's rage was total.

Biglow and Wood were not ready to agree with Parker. The following day, Wood and Biglow rowed the double again, but not in competition. On Sunday, they did what they should have done from the start: They let Biglow stroke, and the boat seemed to take off. Both of them were impressed. On Monday, Parker announced that Frackleton was in the quad and that Wood was out. Hearing the news, Wood asked Biglow if he was encouraged by how well they were doing in the double. Biglow said he was. "Do you want to row at Princeton?" he asked. Biglow said he did.

No one knew what the ramifications of Biglow's agreement might be. Would he have to give up his single title before he took off from the starting line? Or, if he and Wood won, could Biglow have his choice, the single or the double? Wood asked Parker for an opinion. "I don't think you can do it," Parker had answered. He did not say, Wood remembered, "I don't want you to do it." Wood started calling Olympic officials, but no one knew what the rules would be. Wood, as a veteran of Olympic politics past, was sure that Biglow would not have to renounce a title in advance, that the Olympic committee was so anxious for the best scullers to row at Casitas that it would follow what the talent showed. In the meantime, Bouscaren, one of Biglow's oldest friends, angry over Biglow's possible challenge to his own boat, moved out of the room they shared in the Dartmouth dorm and stopped talking to him. Altekruse also moved out on Wood and wrote Biglow a scathing five-page letter in which he stated he was not afraid of Tiff and John and would love to cram the whole thing down their throats on the water. At the same time, Bouscaren and Wood had harsh words.

"You're destroying the camp system," Bouscaren had told Wood.

"The system doesn't work," Wood had answered. "If it did, none of this would have happened."

Harry Parker was furious. He accused Biglow of being manipulative and mischievous out of an old enmity toward Altekruse. (The two, for a variety of reasons, did not get on. A near-fight a year earlier had ended with Biglow's rolling Altekruse's bike down the ramps in front of the Harvard boathouse. Symbolically, the bike fell on its side, short of the water's edge.)

In the camp, the other oarsmen decided that Wood was doing only what anyone in his position should do. Their hostility centered on Biglow. On Tuesday, Biglow, under enormous pressure from Bouscaren, Altekruse and Parker (and knowing that the double was also a challenge to his friend

Paul Enquist), backed off. After Biglow announced his withdrawal, Wood remembered seeing Parker kneeling by the
water's edge at the boat dock, flicking pebbles into the water,
a man apart, unreaching and unreachable.

On Tuesday afternoon, Tiff Wood phoned the American
Stock Exchange and asked to speak to Jim Dietz. Would he
like to row in the double in Princeton this weekend? It was a
call Dietz had been sure he was going to get. In the world of
scullers there were no secrets, and it was widely known that
the camp had turned into a disaster. He had heard earlier in
the week that Wood and Biglow might row the double, and
he had loved that because it meant they would have to rerow
the single trial. Then, when that idea died, he was sure Tiff
would call. Nothing, he told Wood, would please him more.
They would have two days on the water to practice. They
would either make it or not make it quickly. Tiff Wood went
to Harry Parker and told him he was going to row with
Dietz. Parker did not appear angry; but when Wood asked
for the use of a double that belonged to the Olympic committee, Parker said no. Wood mentioned a very good double
owned by Sy Cromwell, who had won a silver at the 1964
Olympics in the double. Doubles were hard to find, and this
one was known throughout the world of rowing as a very
good boat. Cromwell's widow, Gail, had leased it to the
committee for $500, but she was also a friend of Tiff Wood's.
When she had done the leasing, she had thought the unthinkable: What happened if Tiff went to the camp and
didn't make a team boat? Wary that Harry Parker might
put the camp boats out of his reach, she had written the lease
so that it expired a week before the Princeton trials. That
way, if anything went wrong, she could make sure that Tiff
had a boat. Wood now mentioned the Cromwell boat and
the fact that he knew the lease had run out. "I'm not happy
about the situation," Parker said, "and I don't want to talk
about it." So Wood left camp. For fourteen years the interests of the two men had been almost identical, and Wood

184 — David Halberstam

had believed in everything that Harry Parker had said. Now, at this critical moment, their interests completely diverged and their relationship had been torn apart.

Jim Dietz thought that the idea of a Dietz-Wood double was a good one. Although he was worried about the Lewis-Enquist boat, he believed he and Tiff had a very good chance to win. They had nothing to lose and everything to gain. He regarded Wood as the best of the contemporary scullers. He also liked him as a person.

Jim Dietz was the son of a carpenter in the Bronx, and the sound of the New York streets, the blue-collar part of those streets, was still in his voice. His enthusiasm for rowing was almost childlike. "High-School Harry" some of the other rowers called him, with slight condescension, as if he had not entirely grown up. He was aware of how the Ivy Leaguers regarded him. In turn, he felt their snobbery was so pervasive they weren't even aware of it. It was as if a line had been drawn; the rest of them were on one side of it, and he was alone on the other, never completely accepted. During much of his career, some of the scullers had been exceptionally critical of his failure to finish big races strongly. Although physically imposing to them with his height and his immense reach, he often did tire at the end of his races. Some considered the problem as a sign of a lack of character. A few years later, when they all knew a great deal more about genetics and body tissue, they realized that Dietz's failures had not been a lack of character at all, that, despite an unsympathetic genetic structure, one that was probably fifty-fifty in slow-twitch, fast-twitch fiber, Jim Dietz might have been rowing more heroically than any of them. With that knowledge had come a certain grudging new admiration for his career.

Dietz, in turn, thought that unlike most of the other Harvard people, Tiff Wood measured him only on what he was as a man and an oarsman, not on who his parents were and where he had gone to school. He was glad to have one last row with him. They had two days to practice. He knew that

Tiff had not been rowing well, and he knew exactly what he had to do. He had to stop Tiff from rowing with his heart all the time, doing everything with pure courage and strength.

Having rowed well in their first practice, they had both immediately sensed their possibilities. But Dietz, bothered by Wood's roughness, had taken him aside afterward. "Tiff," he said," "if you want to know why you didn't make a boat—I'll tell you. You're just out there hammering the water. You're killing fish, not rowing. Row like you do in practice. Let me set the stroke. The power will always be there." If they could harness their talents, they had a real chance. Dietz might be past his prime, but he was still able to drive a boat very hard.

CHAPTER
TWENTY-TWO

By the time the camp boats arrived at Princeton, Harry Parker was pessimistic about the chances for the Bouscaren-Altekruse double. As far back as the Lucerne regatta, he had been uneasy about Joe Bouscaren's state of mind. In the beginning of the Hanover camp, Bouscaren, possibly because his skills were so readily adaptable to team boats, had been perhaps the most confident oarsman in the camp. But at Lucerne he had started showing signs of anxiety. The day before the first race there, Parker had grabbed him by the shoulders, shaken him gently and told him, "Joe, you're going to wake up tomorrow and feel good and rested and strong. You're going to forget about everything else and you're going to race fast. *Fast*, Joe!" The double, in fact, had done reasonably well; but when the team had returned to Hanover, some of the anxiety also returned. Part of the reason Parker attributed to the furor over the Wood-Biglow double, but even more he sensed that Bouscaren was genuinely concerned about the Lewis-Enquist boat. Already word was filtering back through the rowing channels that Brad and Paul were rowing well. Bouscaren and Altekruse's boat just wasn't moving quickly. They began arguing between themselves, and Bouscaren clearly felt he was being picked on, that Altekruse was blaming him for the boat's problems. He also resented what he thought were Parker's doubts about him: "Are you really ready to race?" Parker kept asking. Finally Bouscaren turned to Parker and Altekruse and told them, "I *do* know how to scull. I am *not* an idiot. You guys have got to stop dumping on me." Going into the race, all the signs of a Bouscaren-Altekruse victory were bad.

The first race, again at Princeton, was to be on Saturday. Although most of the other oarsmen started showing up on Wednesday to work out, Lewis and Enquist appeared on Friday. They were warriors now, confident, almost arrogant. They stayed at a more expensive motel to be away from everyone else. They won their heat on Saturday by six lengths. On Sunday, Tony Johnson, who had helped coach them at Cornell and who was looking out for their interests during this miniature regatta, had gone to see them as they left the boathouse for the race. He wished them good luck. "We're going to kick the shit out of them today," Lewis had said. Johnson was bothered not so much by the obscenity but by the fury with which it had been said. That kind of fury was not necessarily an asset in a race, for it could burn out too quickly, and in a 6-minute race the pair might easily come apart at the end. Oarsmen did not normally talk like that, but Johnson finally decided that both men knew what they were doing, and he did not doubt the outcome.

Lewis and Enquist rowed down to the start and settled into the stake boats that held the sculls at the start of a race. Altekruse and Bouscaren were in the next lane. Lewis heard one of their voices—Altekruse's, he was sure—wishing them good luck. Neither he nor Enquist spoke, nor did they turn their heads. He thought he heard Altekruse say something else. Again they did not acknowledge him. This race was not about friendship. Brad Lewis had found the perfect role for himself, the outsider spurned by authorities, the challenger versus the favorite who had been given all the advantages. He was absolutely comfortable, absolutely ready.

When they had rowed to the stake boat, Joe Bouscaren had heard Charley Altekruse say hello to Lewis and Enquist. When the greeting was unreciprocated, Bouscaren had turned to look at them and seen their faces staring straight ahead, eyes averted. They're really ready, he thought. He wondered if he and Altekruse had the same concentration. He heard Altekruse, annoyed by Lewis and Enquist, telling them, "Hey, come on, you don't have to be like that." He told Altekruse, "Let it go, Charley, it isn't worth it."

Parker, worried about Bouscaren's tendency to burn out at the end, had told them not to go out too high at the start. Bouscaren wanted to go out a little faster; he did not want to spend a championship race behind some very good boats. But at five hundred meters Lewis and Enquist were already ahead by a length, and in the second five hundred they increased the margin. At the thousand-meter mark Bouscaren heard Brad Lewis give a yell of jubilation. To Bouscaren it sounded like an Indian war cry (in reality it was a Japanese judo cry) of absolute triumph. Oh, shit, he thought. He never expected to be down that far that early. The gap widened. Other boats went past them.

Jim Dietz was pleased with the race he and Tiff Wood were rowing. The other boats had been practicing together for weeks and even months, and they had had only two days. Dietz took them out low because he wanted Wood to pick up a rhythm and feel comfortable. The power would come later. The boat moved nicely. The early leaders were Casey Baker and Dan Brisson. Midway in the race, the Enquist-Lewis double made its move. Dietz and Wood gave everything they had, but the other double was too strong. Wood's double had come in second in the time of 6:41.13, some 5 seconds behind the Enquist-Lewis time of 6:35.50. The camp boat came in fourth, at 6:43.10.

The quad race was still ahead. A sculler named Dan Louis had already entered a boat in the hope that some of the defeated double oarsmen might want one more chance. He asked Altekruse and Bouscaren to join him, and they in turn asked Tiff Wood to become part of the instant quad. Wood, his own race finished, was drinking beer when they came by. Recent antagonisms were forgotten, and the sanctity of the camp system was further diminished. "You ask Harry if it's okay," said Altekruse to Wood. Wood went by to see Parker. He would neither, he said, encourage nor discourage the instant quad. Mostly he seemed to shrug his shoulders at the idea. They led for the first twenty strokes. A miracle did not take place, but they had fun. They came in 27 seconds behind the winners. The camp quad also did poorly. "Bloody Sunday," Brad Lewis called it.

Later Tiff Wood went over to thank Dietz. They were oddly pleased with themselves. They were not going to the Olympics—not as boated oarsmen, anyway—but the bitterness of the camp was gone. Dietz had wanted to give it one last try, and he had done that. Wood had wanted to dispel the camp doubt that he was strong but could not row in a team boat, and he had done that. His team boat, with very little notice, had beaten the camp boat. His hopes had not died in Hanover without one last chance on the water.

Dick Cashin, Wood's old Harvard teammate, went over to talk with Bouscaren. He thought that Bouscaren might be disconsolate, but in fact he found him in a very good mood. "So what do you do now?" he asked Bouscaren.

"I'll get on with my life and become a doctor," Bouscaren answered. "It's probably about time, anyway."

"Just getting here is ninety percent of it," said Cashin, who had been eliminated in the pair sweeps the day before. "That's what it's really about."

Harry Parker was in a rage after the trials. He was a man who, in the best of circumstances, took defeat of any kind hard; and a day like this, when both his camp boats had been upset by challengers, was almost a personal humiliation to him.

The entire camp, he thought, had been a disaster. The main problem had been the decision to open the trials to challenges. He had always opposed the idea of trials, but the rowing people from Philadelphia wanted the trials; and rather than a prolonged court fight, he had agreed to the idea the previous fall. Then he had made a critical mistake. He should immediately have canceled participation in the Lucerne races. The trials, once mandated, put too much of a burden on the camp boats and made Lucerne unnecessary. By going to Lucerne, he had lost two or three weeks of critical time and had handed a major psychological advantage to the challengers. If he had stayed in Hanover, his boats would have had more confidence, and the psychology might have been reversed, with the word coming out of Hanover of how well various boats were doing.

He also felt he should have chosen a different method of selection. He should have picked the best quad and then let the oarsmen fight it out among themselves for the two best doubles. Both of those doubles could enter the trials. The best oarsmen would find each other, and the doubles would be good. The oarsmen were shrewd about that. "You're not a sculler if you're not cunning," Brad Lewis liked to say.

But Parker was also aware that he had not coached well. Wounded by the loss of the sweeps to Korzeniowski, by the *way* the committee had done it, he had been so disappointed and distracted that he had never given the sculls his best. Some of the criticism of him by the scullers was legitimate. Although he supported the idea of a national coach who would work with the Olympic rowers free from college responsibilities, he thought that the timing had been a personal betrayal. His oarsmen, the young men he had worked with for the past two years and done all the spadework with, had been given to another coach on the eve of the great events. In the face of this adverse decision, the proper thing to have done was to resign. But he had let his ego get in the way and had allowed a normally positive experience to become a negative one. He had let the scullers down, and that was unthinkable. Understanding his errors and admitting them publicly were among the hardest things he had ever done.

John Biglow had not gone to Princeton for the double trials. He stayed in Hanover rooting for Lewis and Enquist. Paul was his friend, a consistently fair and kind man with whom he had worked out all winter in Seattle. He could not root for Joe and Charley because of all the bitter things that had been said in the camp. He heard the race results by phone. The next day, when Bouscaren came back to Hanover, Biglow wondered if they were still friends. Bouscaren, who had moved out during the height of the tension, had not moved back in. Biglow was in his room when he heard Bouscaren's voice in the hall. Biglow went down the hall; and when Bouscaren offered his hand, Biglow felt an immense sense of relief. "It was tough," Bouscaren said, talking of the trials, "but I have to get on with it. I can't dwell on it." He hung around for a few days, visiting friends. But the day before the new quad and double were supposed to arrive in Hanover, Joe Bouscaren, as quietly as he could, departed.

CHAPTER
TWENTY-THREE

Tiff Wood was chosen as the spare by the Olympic rowing committee. Being the spare in 1976, when he was the backup for the sweeps, had been an exceptionally difficult experience for him. He had never felt so useless in his life. What had made it worse was that everyone around him had been filled with such high purpose. An Olympic camp pulsed with the special intensity of all of those young men and women who had worked so hard and had finally arrived. This time Wood was determined that he would create some kind of role for himself. One of the hardest things for him to come to terms with was the fact that he was rowing exceptionally well. At Hanover, during the practices after the double trials in Princeton, he and Biglow raced regularly against each other, and Wood beat Biglow more often than not. By the time the team went West, first to Berkeley and then to Casitas, he decided that it was not a good idea for him to practice against Biglow, that it might be fun for him but it was not doing John any good.

On his own at Casitas, he shadowed as often as he could the British women's four, which was a very good match for him. The rest of the day was harder. When strangers met him and were excited to discover that he was an Olympic oarsman, he had to explain that he was the *spare* for the scullers. Their disappointment in hearing this was matched by his own in telling it. He had ordered several sets of tickets for his parents, and on the mornings that the scullers were to race he sometimes stood in front of the grandstand, a lonely figure selling tickets that were no longer needed. That was not exactly a memorable Olympic experience. Getting rides back and forth between Casitas and the dorms at Cal Santa Barbara was also difficult. The Americans had a van to transport their oarsmen; and while the van might wait for oarsmen and coaches and coxes, it did not wait for the spare. If he was not exactly on time, the van left without him.

He felt as if everyone knew that he belonged but did not belong. His only hope was to capitalize on someone else's misfortune, but no one showed the slightest sign of becoming sick. He neither avoided nor sought out Harry Parker. The rupture between them was real, at least on Wood's part. It might be that Parker was willing to patch up their split, but Tiff Wood was still wounded. When he thought back to the summer he decided the critical moment—when he did not make the double—had come and passed without his even realizing it. Given the immediacy of the pressures to get ready for Lucerne and the difficulty of adjusting to the quad, he had had virtually no chance of making the quad. He faulted Harry for not making sure that more combinations were tried for the double, even at the expense of not doing well at Lucerne. The entire process had been too casual and disorganized. The other possibility that ran through his mind was that Harry had never thought that highly of his talents in the first place.

The hardest part of the camp for Harry Parker had been in trying to find a place for Tiff Wood. From the moment that Tiff did not win the singles trial, Parker had a special dilemma: a favorite and special oarsman who to his mind did not easily fit into team boats. At Hanover he had hoped that Tiff would do well in the double. Wood had rowed well with Paul Enquist, and Parker and Allsopp had given serious consideration to the pair. In the end they had decided that the Bouscaren-Altekruse boat was better. Parker did not believe he had been negligent in dealing with Wood. If anything, one of the things that had slowed down the camp had been Parker's concern about a place for him. But Parker also admitted that he had not done as good a job in trying all the combinations as he might have and that some of Wood's (and the other rowers') complaints were more than legitimate. But one of the problems was that each of the top oarsmen thought the selection process should revolve around him. That made it a matter of perspective, for the job of a coach was not to take care of individual oarsmen, no matter how much in his heart he rooted for one of them, but to find the fastest boats possible.

Selecting boats was even more difficult for an Olympic team than for a college one. In college, a coach's decision was cushioned by the fact that an oarsman was part of the larger community of the school and had to accept what was best for that community. But on an Olympic team, each oarsman was out for himself. Denying Tiff Wood a boat was the hardest thing Parker had done in his entire career as a coach. He hated being a part of it. The sight of Wood at the Olympics, apart, all that talent wasted, was a very painful one for him.

CHAPTER
TWENTY-FOUR

John Biglow was excited about being in the Olympic camp. He loved being surrounded by all these athletes who shared his sense of purpose and who had sacrificed years of their lives to be here. He loved talking to Romanian coach Victor Mociani, though in fact they could not talk at all, since Biglow did not speak Romanian and Mociani did not speak English. But Mociani seemed to like him, calling his name enthusiastically and trying hard, through a kind of instant sign language, to communicate some idea of friendship. In that moment it seemed as if all Romanian people could be friends with all Americans.

Biglow knew many of the other oarsmen in the camp from previous regattas. Pertti Karppinen was there, not so much aloof as apart, a man clearly troubled by his lack of languages. But he always shook hands and nodded his head to Biglow when they met. Peter-Michael Kolbe, to Biglow's surprise, was friendly to everyone this time, but Biglow was wary of Kolbe. He was being friendly to Americans now that he was in America, but when the races had been held in Germany, he had been distant and uncommunicative.

The schedule for the single scullers was brutal. The heats were on Tuesday; the reps, for those who did not win their heats, were on Wednesday; the semifinal was on Thursday;

and the final was on Sunday. That might mean three days of
back-to-back racing if he did not qualify for the semi in his
first race. Nor was he likely to. He drew, in his heat, both
Kolbe and Karppinen. Part of Biglow was slightly shaken by
that, but a larger part was delighted because it gave him a
chance to row against both of them without the pressure of it
being a final.

He went out very quickly in the heat, which was unusual
for him, but he gradually fell behind. Kolbe had taken the
early lead; and then, in the last few hundred meters, Karppinen made a move. At that point ABC, covering the race,
broke for a commercial, leaving the scullers suspended in
midrace. The commercial was for McDonald's and featured
a man who orders some twenty fish sandwiches for his
friends. They also all have Cokes. Back on Casitas, Kolbe did
not contest Karppinen. This would be Karppinen's race
without a challenge. Biglow, falling farther and farther back,
was struggling. Known for his powerful finishing sprints, he
appeared tired at the end. Karppinen beat him by 10 seconds; Kolbe, easing himself in, by 3. (Someone had seen
Kolbe watching the videotape afterward, and he had nar-
rated the race carefully to friends. "Now, this is where I stop
racing," Kolbe had said, pointing to a moment in the last
few hundred meters. A young Dutch woman had asked him
why he had stopped racing. "I don't have to beat Karppinen
every time I race. Only once," he had answered.)

Biglow was disappointed with the way he had rowed: He
was not even competitive with Karppinen and Kolbe. It was
clear that what Biglow had feared from the start was true.
The best he could hope for was a bronze. When an American
journalist asked if he thought he could get a gold, he replied,
"I expect to get a bronze, but I had hoped to do better."

The rep the next day was relatively easy. All he had to do
was be among the top three finishers to make the semi. He
wanted to win it, however, because Harry Parker had
charted and projected the semis and he drew an easier semi
if he won. He finished first handily, beating Gary Reid of

New Zealand by 5 seconds, but he had not been able to coast through on three-quarter pressure. That had given him a place in the semifinal against Kolbe and Ricardo Ibarra of Argentina. Ibarra, who had won his heat, had had a day off; for Biglow, the semi was his third race in three days. Biglow knew that he was a good endurance athlete, that he did better as a regatta went on and as fatigue overtook the others. But that was only if everyone was subjected to the same amount of stress.

In the semi he felt tired. Kolbe and Ibarra shot out quickly and were gone from him in the early part of the race. At five-hundred meters he was sixth. The work was harder than it should have been. For the first time he began to worry about making the final. Slowly he passed some of the oarsmen. At fifteen hundred meters he was even with Bengt Nilsson of Sweden, whom he had expected to beat easily. Then Nilsson began to fade. The last part of the race simply seemed to last longer and take more energy than Biglow had planned. In the end he finished third, 2.5 seconds behind Kolbe, who was first, and behind Ibarra, who was second. Biglow was not pleased with himself, but he had made the final and he had two days to rest.

CHAPTER
TWENTY-FIVE

Brad Lewis had been only momentarily exhilarated after winning in the challenge boat at Princeton. He and Paul Enquist were the American double. Lewis was still angry about what had happened in the camp, and he flew out to California immediately. He did not want to go to another camp in Hanover, a place he had come to hate. Even worse, it was run by Harry Parker, a coach who had bypassed him in the selection process. There was some talk that he would practice in California alone in a single and join up with Enquist only at the last minute in California. Enquist was upset; it was as if Lewis had undergone another personality change after the race, becoming unreachable again. Enquist, who headed for Hanover, kept talking to Lewis, who eventually agreed to come East to practice with Enquist and to allow Parker, among others, to oversee their training.

However aloof he may have been, Lewis was excited by the fact that he was going to compete in the Olympics. In 1976, as a young man just out of college, he had gone to Montreal, believing that this was probably the one chance he would have to see an Olympiad on the North American continent. He had gloried in watching the Olympic rowers. They seemed at once so near, for he had rowed in college, and yet, by their achievements, so distant. They were the best in the world. He did not have a lot of money, but Montreal was not expensive. He had bought a $3 standing-room ticket to watch the final of the single sculls, in which Karppinen had beaten Kolbe at the end. It had been a magnificent race in which Kolbe, the reigning world champion and a great sculler, had been beaten by Karppinen, who was then virtually unknown.

What Lewis remembered about the race was that Karppinen had never before beaten any of his principal opponents. Lewis and Enquist had not beaten any of the principal crews either; but they were good enough to beat all of them, and they were going to row as aggressively as possible. Lewis had looked carefully at videotapes of Lucerne and last year's world championships, checking out the stroke ratings at which each double had rowed and which crews were most likely to challenge them. He decided that Paul and he in 1983 had probably been as good as most of their European competitors; but because they simply had not realized it, they had not rowed with enough confidence.

Looking at the film of Lucerne, where in back-to-back races Altekruse and Bouscaren had taken fourth and fifth, he concluded that the Americans had rowed too conservatively. Since the East Germans, who had had the best double at Lucerne, would not row at Lake Casitas, the West Germans, the Canadians and the Yugoslavs were likely to be the principal competition. Lewis made up his mind that he and Enquist would fill the shoes of the East Germans. The men from that double were big and strong, as were Lewis and Enquist; and when they rowed, they concentrated not so much on the quickness of the rating but on a beat that allowed them maximum power. Like the East Germans, they would use a stroke in which the oar spent a briefer time in the water and a longer time on the recovery. That seemed to suit their size and their power better. There was no reason why Paul and he could not win; there was no double that was beyond their reach. He continued to work on Enquist's motivation, buying him a three-foot inflatable shark and lettering the words "Stay Hungry" on it.

Enquist and he were warriors now. They would not hobnob with other rowers from other countries. Warriors stayed apart and did not fraternize. If they were on the water at the same time as another double, even if it was a time when they were just paddling, they would pass the other boat. Right before the first trial, Lewis tried to think of something else warriors would do. If the West Germans were the enemy, the leading double to beat, a warrior would piss on the flagpole that carried their flag. He told Enquist he was going to do it.

"Try not to get arrested and put in jail," Enquist said. "It's a little late for me to learn to row with Tiff."

CHAPTER
TWENTY-SIX

Harry Parker was one of the coaches working with Lewis and
Enquist during the Olympics, and he was aware of Lewis's
resentment. That did not bother him. What bothered him
was the knowledge that as a coach he had handled Brad
Lewis poorly and had fallen into the game that Brad set for
his coaches. That was the game of rejection, and it almost
guaranteed that no coach could over a very long period succeed with Lewis and that he would have to be by himself.
The only thing Lewis responded to, Parker decided bela-
tedly, was complete support and constant reassurance, two
things Parker had not given him. In the first place, it was
alien for Parker to treat oarsmen that way, and in the second
place, he had lacked time. In 1983, he believed, he had handled Lewis well, particularly on the days when, unlike most
high-quality oarsmen, he simply had not wanted to work
out. The one thing that had bothered Parker after the 1983
season was his sense that Brad had been satisfied just to
make the finals in the World and had not tried hard enough
at the end. A year later, Parker realized he had completely
underestimated the real rage and passion within Lewis. But
it had taken his own decisions at the camp to trigger that
rage. He had done Lewis, however involuntarily, the great

favor of casting him perfectly, as the avenger who had been wronged by the system.

But Lewis had been difficult to evaluate at the camp, performing well if the mood suited him and if he was paired with someone he liked, and not performing close to his possibilities if he was paired with someone he didn't like. Parker had paired him early on with Enquist and had expected that boat to do well. When it did not, Parker suspected that Lewis regarded Enquist, his partner from the past, as somehow beneath him. On another occasion he had been placed in a double with Charley Altekruse. From the start, Parker knew it was trouble. Lewis sat in the boat, head down, not looking up. He did not speak. They rowed two pieces, both of them poorly, and took a break. "I think we have an attitude problem in the boat," said Altekruse.

Parker decided that part of the problem with Brad was that on the basis of the singles trial he felt that he had proven himself superior to most of the scullers and that because of that superiority he did not need to perform anew each day. But this was an Olympic camp, and the competition was savage. Nothing was granted to past performances.

To Parker, Lewis had represented a coach's nightmare. Do you pick and project Brad on the basis of his best performances or on the basis of his more dilatory ones, on the days when he was ready to row or when he was not ready to row? Those were hard choices.

CHAPTER
TWENTY-SEVEN

In the first Olympic heat, Lewis and Enquist were competing against the West Germans and the Norwegians. The West Germans went out quickly and took a big lead. Lewis and Enquist had in their boat strokemeters that showed at what rate they were going; and they were not able to keep the stroke as high as they had wanted, at a thirty-four. At a thousand meters there was perhaps a length of open water between them and the West Germans. Lewis and Enquist began to take the stroke up, and they closed hard and fast, finishing only 1.5 seconds behind. Lewis was pleased with the finish but not with the race. Despite their vows, they still had not rowed aggressively enough. It had been one thing to decide in advance at what rate they would row and quite another thing to sustain it in the water. Lewis attributed their failing to inexperience. It was only the seventh time he and Enquist had raced as a double, while some of the European pairs had raced together a hundred times.

When the double had not rowed as well as Lewis expected in the first heat, he had become upset. Enquist tipped off Parker that Brad was brooding about coming in second; and Dave Grant, who had coached at Orange Coast College and knew Lewis well, and Parker tried to help him regain his

204 — David Halberstam

confidence. The support for Brad, Grant said, had to be complete. "Harry," he added, "sometimes those who need love the most deserve it the least." Parker and Grant repeatedly told the two men how well they had done in the heat and how strongly they had come on in the second half of the race. The future, they emphasized, belonged to the two Americans.

Because Lewis and Enquist had taken second in the heat, they had to go to the repechage. For Lewis that was the truly terrifying race. He wanted above all else to make the final and to medal, but if they did not do well in the rep, that was it. Only two boats from their rep would make the final, and the rep was critical for some of the European doubles who, if they did not make the final, would lose their funding for the coming year. That meant the rep would be rowed all-out in a way usually reserved for a final. Lewis and Enquist decided to lead from start to finish. The Yugoslavs, their strongest competition, had the same idea. The Yugoslavs were a little ahead after the first five hundred meters, still ahead by a little at a thousand. At the fifteen-hundred mark the Americans took the lead and won by 2 seconds. They were in the final, and their confidence was growing.

CHAPTER
TWENTY-EIGHT

On the Sunday of the finals, Tiff Wood got up very early. This was race day, but he was not going to race. He was full of purpose and absolutely without purpose in that which meant the most to him. He had always planned to make the Olympic race his last one and then retire. Earlier in the week he had talked with Pat Walter, the Canadian spare who was also a world-class oarsman, about having a race among the spares. It would liven things up a little, and it might give him a greater sense of belonging. They talked of getting the West German spare to join them. Walter was amenable to the idea, but he told Wood the choice was his. In the end Wood decided that, since this was his last row, he did not want anything to disrupt his thoughts. This was a moment to have by himself. Walter sympathized, but in order to have some sense of excitement, they decided that Wood would go out exactly two minutes before Walter. That way they could clock each other and maintain some element of pressure.

It was an odd row. When Wood went out, the weather was clear and at the thousand-meter mark the fog came in so thick that he could not see. As he rowed the last thousand meters wrapped in fog, he thought of what might have been; and he told himself that the important thing was to deal

with his disappointment as a man, to be graceful and generous. That was what rowing was all about. It demanded so
much in preparation that even if he fell short of his goals, he
was not diminished as a person. He told himself this, but
he found it hard to take much comfort from his own words.
He had been a member of three Olympic teams without
rowing one stroke. When he finished the two thousand
meters, he waited for Walter. Two minutes passed. There
was no sign of Walter. The Canadian, hit even harder by the
fog, came in about 30 seconds later. No race there. Then
Wood went back and started taking apart the rigging of his
boat. He did it just when he knew John Biglow was going to
race. He was immensely fond of John, but he could not bear
to watch him row in the singles. It was simply too painful.

CHAPTER
TWENTY-NINE

Biglow's rowing was proving an enigma both to himself and to his coaches. Harry Parker was convinced that Biglow's back was the source of his troubles. The power that a few years ago had been there and so readily available could no longer be summoned. It was a physical problem, but it showed up on no tests. Yet during the last few weeks of practice, Biglow, after doing his usual five-hundred-meter pieces, told Parker, "I just feel weak." Biglow found himself saying the same things during the Olympics. The difference seemed to be in his legs. He was not the same sculler he had been in 1981 and 1982. He was trying mightily and, in Parker's opinion, was being very brave. Things he had once done he no longer could do. Still Parker thought he had an excellent chance for the bronze.

After racing Tuesday, Wednesday and Thursday, John finally had some time in which to rest. His body was exhausted, and he hoped the others felt as tired. On Saturday, the night before the final, Harry Parker dropped by his room, in part to talk strategy, but in part, Biglow suspected, to let him know that Parker was with him. He realized that in the final Karppinen and Kolbe were beyond his reach. His two main competitors for the bronze were Ibarra of Argentina and Robert Mills of Canada. Biglow had beaten both of them on occasion and had lost to them on occasion. He was confident of beating Mills but more worried about Ibarra because Ibarra had beaten him in the semifinal. He had decided to key as much as he could on Ibarra. I will row my own race, he had vowed to himself. I can make only my own boat go fast. I cannot slow anyone else down. I will not think of the other boats nor let them disrupt me.

Rowing his own race meant he planned to be behind at the thousand-meter mark and then start charging. That was the style he was most comfortable with. But the others went out very quickly and he had, even within his own game plan, gotten a terrible start. At the five-hundred-meter mark he was much farther behind than he intended to be. He was sixth, and the only boat he could even see was that of the Greek, Konstantinos Kontomanolis, and he was behind that. By the thousand-meter-mark he had pulled slightly ahead of Kontomanolis. But the race was turning into a disaster.

Far ahead of him, a magnificent duel was beginning to take shape. Kolbe, in what was almost surely his last chance for a gold, had taken a considerable lead over the Finn. Karppinen was battling back, but this time Kolbe was not cracking. But that was another country. Farther back in the third five hundred, Biglow sighted Ibarra and Mills, who, to his surprise, was ahead of Ibarra. Biglow went after Ibarra and came through him in the third five hundred. That left Mills but Mills seemed too far ahead. Later he found out that the official time showed him 6.2 seconds behind Mills with five hundred meters to go, a huge difference. For a moment he thought of not even trying, but he knew he simply had to try, this was the last race of his life, and so he sprinted. He did not, as he sometimes did during a sprint, shorten his stroke. He simply tried to feed more power in. In the last three hundred meters, he seemed to fly; the boat was almost lifted out of the water, and he kept closing and closing on Mills. Ahead of him Karppinen was finally making his own surge, a powerful, determined challenge, not so much taking the beat up but feeding more power in; and

Kolbe was trying to hold him off. The race might have been the greatest of Kolbe's life. For a moment it appeared Kolbe would hold the Finn off this time. Kolbe led by .86 second with 250 meters to go. But in the last hundred meters Karppinen, just on sheer muscle, passed him, winning by 1.95 seconds.

Biglow's surge came too late. If he had started 150 meters earlier, he might have succeeded. But Mills took third, 1.62 seconds ahead of him. That meant Biglow had cut 4.6 seconds off Mills with his closing drive. He finished fourth and missed the medal. The first thing he felt was relief that he did not have to race again, that he would never have to worry again about doing well. Then he worried briefly whether he could have rowed just a little harder, reached back for a little more. Some of his disappointment was short-lived, and some of it lasted long after the race was over. It was not just that he could not compete at the very highest level with Karppinen and Kolbe but that he had not improved in the three years since he had won his first world bronze. If anything, he might have slipped a little.

At the ceremonies, when he saw Robert Mills standing on the platform with Karppinen and Kolbe, getting the bronze, a wave of intense jealousy swept over him. Biglow was stunned by how much he wanted the recognition that Mills was receiving. Just then, Harry Parker came over to the dock. Biglow was surprised to see Parker there. He did not really know, he realized, how Parker felt about him. After all, Parker no longer had to feign any interest in him; there was nothing more that Biglow could do for Parker, no more medals he could bring him. Perhaps Parker liked him and believed in him more than he had realized. Harry Parker was smiling, which also surprised Biglow, and he was unusually gentle. He reached out and rubbed Biglow's hair.

"That was a tough one," he said.

"Harry, I think I raced as well as I could have," Biglow said.

"John, you were ready to race today," Parker said.

At that moment it was the nicest thing Biglow could hear. He felt miserable. He sat with a friend named Seth Bauer, a former Yale coxswain and now cox of the Olympic eight, and shook his head bitterly. "I can't believe it; I just *didn't* race," he said. "I can't believe it—I just let it slip away." He told Bauer he knew he wasn't moving quickly enough in the first part of the race, but he had been unable to do anything about it. After the race he went into the stands to visit with his family. Charley McIntyre, his old friend and coach, was there, and McIntyre had told him he had rowed well, very well, that he had flown down the course in the last five hundred. Praise from McIntyre was not easy to come by, and Biglow was pleased. Later, looking at the pictures of those moments, he was stunned by how happy he looked. His dream had ended, he had just taken fourth, he had missed a medal and yet the photos showed a relaxed, surprisingly happy young man. He was sure that what showed on his face was the relief that he did not have to row again, not so much the rowing itself, the practices, the workouts, but that he no longer had to live up to other people's hopes and expectations.

CHAPTER
THIRTY

Brad Lewis and Paul Enquist were getting on well, although they were not, as an outsider might have supposed, rooming together. They had decided that their temperaments were too different and that the possibilities of tensions far outweighed any presumed benefits. Lewis was rooming with Tiff Wood, Enquist with Biglow. After the semi, Lewis and Enquist studied the split sheet, which gave the times for each boat over the various increments of the race. They were clearly the fastest boat over the last thousand meters. Their problem was not to fall too far behind in the early part of the race.

They raced the final on Sunday. The Belgians went out early, at a very high cadence, and took a commanding lead. At a thousand meters they were two lengths ahead. In the boat Enquist, who was heavier, stroked so that the lighter Lewis could be in the bow. Lewis did all the talking. They had reduced their strategy to code words. "Quick hands," Lewis said, which meant get your hands away from your body as quickly as you can. That the Belgians were ahead did not bother him. At this point in days past, he would have panicked and changed his racing tactics. Instead he and Enquist rowed their race. "Nobody beats us," Lewis said as they rowed. At fifteen hundred meters the Belgians still had a length lead. "Zealand," Lewis said, a trigger word for New Zealand, which meant sit up a little higher in the boat and shorten up your stroke, as the New Zealand oarsmen did. For the first time Lewis could now see the Belgians in his peripheral vision. They were falling back. "We're getting them," he told Enquist. With about four hundred meters to go, he and Enquist took a power twenty. That pulled them even. "East Germans," Lewis said, which meant sit up even higher in your seat the way the East Germans do. It was a way of fighting sloppiness when they were both tired. But Lewis and Enquist felt fine now. Lewis knew they had the Belgians, knew their boat was going to win. He and Enquist stayed even for the next fifteen strokes. With twenty strokes left in the race, the American double pulled ahead. "We've got them," Lewis said. "Real nice, real pretty now." He did not want either of them to blow the race by overreaching when they already had it won. They won by 1.5 seconds. He and Enquist had medaled, a dream fulfilled. More than that, they had won the gold. That was beyond the dream. It was the ninth double race of Lewis's life. Brad Lewis is an Olympic gold-medal winner, he thought. The record books will always say that. Brad Lewis, Corona del Mar, California. All that work, all that work is really worth something. Everything he had wanted to happen had happened. All his weirdness would now be seen as genius. Harry Parker was there congratulating him and pounding him on the back. He had never seen Harry so happy.

He stood on the platform receiving the medal. Enquist, who always looked quiet and stoic, looked quiet and stoic. But Lewis, who never smiled, smiled and pumped his hands over his head like a victorious boxer. He took the flowers a young girl gave him and handed them to his sister and took the gold medal and handed it to his mother.

A few days later, Brad Lewis and Paul Enquist received a small package from Mike Livingston, who had been traveling with his family in Hawaii. It had been mailed before the finals. Inside was a small plastic shark. The note said, "Go for the gold. The great white shark strikes in the last thousand meters. Do not be denied."

CHAPTER
THIRTY-ONE

Joe Bouscaren was on duty that Sunday at Virginia Mason Hospital in Seattle, where he was just beginning his internship. He had watched as much of the Olympics as he could, and he had been surprised by how moved he had been by them. They were not just a sporting event, the biggest regatta of all time, but something bigger, something part athletic, part spiritual, part theatrical. Their sheer size had mesmerized him, and suddenly he wanted desperately to be a part of them. Up until then he was sure that he had dealt well with his disappointment. He had looked back on his defeat as rationally as he could: He had done his best, he had prepared as well as he could and he had lost. He did not believe that Lewis and Enquist had won because they had harnessed and tuned what was superior strength. He believed that the critical moment for him and Altekruse was their flight to Lucerne to race in the international regatta there. They had peaked too early in their training, and Lucerne had cost them nearly two weeks in time on the water. He still believed that he and Altekruse had formed the best double that year. They had beaten Lewis and Enquist during the camp.

That Sunday morning, Bouscaren was popping in and out of hospital rooms as best he could, and rushing back to a television set so he could watch the rowing finals. He watched Lewis and Enquist win with an odd mixture of regret and disappointment. When they were standing on the podium and he saw the smile on Lewis's face, Bouscaren thought, I should be there. Suddenly he was angry that Brad and Paul had gotten a chance and he had not; he felt that he and Altekruse deserved it as much as they did. He was also finding that it was harder to let go of rowing than he had expected. He was working hard staying in shape. He had taken a house on Lake Washington, three miles from the hospital. The way to the hospital was uphill, and he roller-skied to work every day, returning at night by running. He was going to buy a kayak so he could work out on the water daily (the sculling facilities were too distant). He was thinking very seriously of rowing again, but if he did, it would be for 1988 and the Olympics.

THIRTY-TWO

John Biglow was getting ready for medical school at Dartmouth. He wrote letters to all his friends and enclosed Olympic rowing pins for most of them. The letter to his old friend Dan Goldberg, the former Yale coxswain, said in part, "It is not going to be easy to give up this sport. I am satisfied about the single, i.e., knowing my potential, but have unknown potential in the double and quad." It was the letter of a man who had not completely decided to give up rowing. Any number of friends offered him videotapes of the final of the single scull. He did not accept any of the offers. He had heard that Kolbe, watching the videotapes of the final seconds when Karppinen had rowed through him, had burst into tears; and for the first time he found himself sympathetic to Kolbe. Biglow did not need to see the race again. He remembered perfectly—too perfectly, in fact—how it had gone. To watch it again would only be to feel the pain and disappointment once more, an exercise as pointless as watching a videotape of the 1979 Harvard-Yale race. The farther he was from the Olympic race, the less disappointed he became and the more relieved that the stress was removed. What bothered him most now was Tiff Wood. He worried whether Tiff felt he should have rowed the single, and he worried that Tiff believed he might have won the bronze had he rowed. But there was nothing Biglow could do about that. Sometimes he thought he might give one more try to rowing, in the team boats. He also thought he would write Mitch Lewis, Brad's cousin, to find out a little more about Mitch's weight-lifting program.

CHAPTER
THIRTY-THREE

Brad Lewis enjoyed immensely the grand tour of the United States with the other American Olympic medalists, even though being a gold medalist in a sport as eccentric as rowing did not increase his fame very much. The other rowers knew that he had won a gold, and some local papers paid attention. Other than that, the feeling of pleasure came entirely from within. What was it, he asked a friend, that Andy Warhol had said about fame in America? That it lasted for fifteen minutes? That was probably right. On this tour he quickly learned how to achieve instant fame. "All you have to do," he said, "is stand just behind the gymnasts at any ceremony. The cameras go wherever they go."

EPILOGUE

A few months after the Olympics, to everyone's relief, Brad Lewis quit his job at the Wells Fargo bank. The last thing he intended to be was a banker. He did some lecturing on his Olympic experiences, and he enjoyed that. He particularly liked showing the cassette of ABC's videotape coverage of the final. During the narration Curt Gowdy, who knew, of course, of the outcome long before he began his commentary, described the American double as being behind at a thousand meters. "But Lewis and Enquist aren't worried," Gowdy said. "Bullshit," came Lewis's voice from the back of the room. The audience loved it. He bought a word processor and started to write a book about his experiences. In the fall he wanted to row with Tiff Wood in a double, but Tiff did not seem that interested. Lewis was going to stay with sculling a little longer, and he hoped to row at Henley in the single in 1985.

John Biglow decided on Dartmouth Medical School over Penn and knew immediately that he had made the right choice. He loved the rural setting and all the outdoor activities that Hanover offered. He was not rowing for the moment, and he was not sure that he would return to serious competition in the spring. He took an elective course on stress taught by a psychiatrist and enjoyed it immensely, particularly when his fellow students, during classroom debate, told him that he was often difficult for them to deal with. He had a tendency, they said, to ask very intimate questions of them while not revealing very much of himself. That did not surprise him very much. He was thinking very seriously of being a small-town doctor.

Joe Bouscaren found that he wanted quite badly to compete in the 1988 Olympics. He also received something he had long desired, an offer from New York Hospital for Special Surgery for his residency. It was one of the most sought-after places at one of the great hospitals in America; indeed, he had often had nightmares in the past year that somehow his name would not be on the list of those accepted. But the rowing fever still burned, and very much to his surprise he found himself considering turning down this cherished appointment and instead taking the most ordinary of positions in an emergency room at a hospital near a great rowing center. The advantage was simple enough: In the emergency room he would work long but set hours, and it would allow him a very free hand to continue with his rowing. Word that he was considering making the decision stunned his friends. When Tony Johnson heard of the possibility, he simply shook his head. "He's really competitive, isn't he?" Johnson said. Bouscaren pondered this choice for several weeks, and in the end he opted for the residency at the Hospital for Special Surgery; but the incident showed how torn he was by the idea of the 1988 Olympics.

Tiff Wood was still undergoing withdrawal symptoms from rowing. He worked out very little on the Charles, but in the fall he did enter the Head of the Charles, coming in second behind Andy Sudduth. Sudduth, who had rowed in the eight at the Olympics, was now seen by the other scullers as the rising star among their group. Wood was frustrated by the fact that he had not done better, but he was wary of committing himself to a more ambitious program. He and Kristy Aserlind announced their engagement, and in mid-December a large engagement party was held in their honor. Tiff Wood pondered one question for a long time and then decided to ask Harry Parker to the party. Harry remained, for all the pain of the past year, an important part of his life.

ACKNOWLEDGMENTS

I would like to thank Kathryn Reith and Ellen Haskins of the U.S. Rowing Association for assistance far beyond the call of duty; my friend Nancy Medeiros for typing my notes; and, for their time, Charley Altekruse, Kristy Aserlind, Seth Bauer, John Biglow, Nancy Biglow, Joe Bouscaren, Mike Bouscaren, Joe Burk, Dick Cashin, Gene Clapp, Meredith Clapp, Sean Colgan, Frank Cunningham, Richard Davis, Jim Dietz, Paul Enquist, Bob Ernst, Andy Fisher, Curtis Fleming, Dan Goldberg, Fritz Hagerman, Fritz Hobbs, Bruce Ibbetson, Tony Johnson, Stanley N. Katz (class of 1921 Bicentennial Professor of the History of Law and Liberty at Princeton, and coxswain of the 1955 Dunster House crew), Kathy Keeler, Steve Kiesling, Brad Lewis, Dave Lewis, Mitch Lewis, Cleve Livingston, Mike Livingston, Virginia Livingston, Ed Markey, Charley McIntyre, Tom Mendenhall, Paula Oberstein, Harry Parker, John Powers, Peter Raymond, Harrison Salisbury, Al Shealy, Gregg Stone, Mike Vespoli, Jane Wood, Pamela Wood, Richard Wood and Tiff Wood.